THEESSENTIALSOF
HIPHOPDRUMMING

Master The Art of Breakbeats, New Jack Swing, Boom Bap, Drunk Grooves & Trap

GIUSEPPE**GRONDONA**

FUNDAMENTAL**CHANGES**

The Essentials of Hip-Hop Drumming

Master The Art of Breakbeats, New Jack Swing, Boom Bap, Drunk Grooves & Trap

ISBN: 978-1-78933-467-8

Published by **www.fundamental-changes.com**

Copyright © 2025 Giuseppe Grondona

Edited by Joseph Alexander

www.fundamental-changes.com

Instagram: **FundamentalChanges**

Contents

About the Author

Born in Bari and now based in London, Giuseppe Grondona has built a career as a performer and university lecturer in the UK since 2005. Over two decades, he has collaborated with a diverse range of artists, including Tormento (Sottotono), the Maurizio Grondona Group, Bosco De Oliveira (Airto Moreira, Sade, Terry Callier, Hamish Stuart, Kate Bush), Femi Temowo (Wynton Marsalis, George Benson, Amy Winehouse), Simon Carter (Jamiroquai), Svetlana Vassileva (Moby), Annabel Williams (X Factor, Britain's Got Talent), John Wheatcroft (Carl Palmer), Andrew McKinney (James Taylor Quartet), and TM Stevens (James Brown).

His career spans international tours, studio recordings, live TV performances, and appearances at major festivals, including the Ealing Jazz Festival, the London Drum Show, UK Bass Day, Untold Festival, the Los Angeles Indie-Music/Film International Summit, and the Lucca Summer Festival.

After graduating from the N. Piccinni Conservatoire in Bari in 2001, he quickly moved into teaching, securing positions at some of the UK's most prestigious popular music institutions. He began at Drumtech in 2005, moved to Tech Music School in 2009, and joined BIMM London in 2012, where he currently serves as Lead Lecturer for the BMus in Popular Music Performance.

Throughout his academic career, he has mentored and guided over a thousand students, many of whom have gone on to perform with major artists. Notable alumni include Simon Tellier (Pet Shop Boys, Jason Derulo), Fabio De Oliveira (George Clinton, Jacob Collier, George Ezra, Jordan Rakei, Soweto Kinch), Rufus Taylor (Queen, The Darkness), Jamie Murray (Beat Replacement, Tim Lefebvre), Vicky O'Neon (Anastacia), and Naomi Forbes (Paloma Faith).

Introduction

My journey into hip-hop drumming began in the early '90s when I heard my first hip-hop track and was immediately captivated by its unique feel and groove. Coming from a jazz and fusion background, this was an entirely new world for me, but it was one I was instantly drawn to. The Roots were my gateway, and Questlove's signature grooves also had a major impact on my playing. As I dug deeper, I discovered J Dilla, whose innovative approach to swing changed my entire understanding of rhythm.

To truly understand these styles, I immersed myself in understanding the grooves of drum machines, particularly the Akai MPC. I studied sampling techniques, experimented with swing functions, and recreated classic beats from scratch. This hands-on approach helped me to bridge the precision of digital production with the organic feel of live drumming.

Later, as an educator, I developed methods to effectively teach these ideas to my students. One of my former students, Matteo D'Ignazi, has since become one of the most sought-after hip-hop and jazz-hop drummers in Italy and played a key role in developing this book.

With Matteo's support, I wrote this book as a comprehensive guide for drummers looking to master hip-hop grooves across different subgenres, from New Jack Swing and Boom Bap to Neo-Soul and Trap. My goal is to provide technical exercises, historical context, and stylistic breakdowns, so you don't just play the beats but understand their origins and evolution too.

I hope this book inspires you to experiment, innovate, and make these grooves your own – just like the legends of hip-hop drumming did before us.

The Evolution of Hip-Hop

In this book we'll follow the chronology of hip-hop's evolution to explore each major style and its defining drumming techniques. The journey begins with Breakbeats (the foundation of early hip-hop), before moving through New Jack Swing, Boom Bap, Neo-Soul and Trap. Each chapter takes a look at the history, stylistic characteristics, and technical elements that shaped these grooves, and provides detailed exercises to help you play them with authenticity and feel.

Understanding hip-hop drumming goes beyond learning patterns. The rhythms in this book are deeply connected to sampling culture, drum machine programming, and the art of groove manipulation. By studying how producers crafted these beats, and how live drummers adapted them, you will develop a broader perspective on hip-hop's rhythmic language.

What you're reading is the result of years of playing, studying, and teaching. It is designed to give you not only the technical skills to play hip-hop, but the insight to feel the music in a deeper way.

Get the Audio

The audio files for this book are available to download for free from www.fundamental-changes.com. The link is in the top right-hand corner. Click Download Audio and choose Drums. Select the title of this book from the menu and complete the form to get your audio.

We recommend that you download the files directly to your computer (not to your tablet or phone) and extract them there before adding them to your media library. If you encounter any difficulty, we provide technical support within 24 hours via the contact form.

Tag us for a share on Instagram: **FundamentalChanges**

Chapter One: Hip-Hop – Historical Overview

Hip-hop has had several pivotal moments in its history, both as a musical genre and a cultural movement. Pinpointing an exact origin is difficult due to differing theories, but it is widely accepted that hip-hop emerged in the Bronx, a predominantly African American, low-income district in New York City.

On August 11, 1973, Clive "Kool Herc" Campbell, a Jamaican-born DJ, hosted what is now considered the first hip-hop party at 1520 Sedgwick Avenue. At the time, hip-hop was still taking shape. DJs experimented with turntables, blending funk and soul records to create extended instrumental breaks that encouraged dancing. Vocals had yet to become a core element of the music.

Hip-hop developed as a response to the violence, poverty, and racial marginalisation affecting young people in urban ghettos. It revolves around four key elements: deejaying, rapping (also known as MCing), graffiti art, and B-boying (breakdancing).

The terms rap and hip-hop are often used interchangeably, but they are not the same. Rap refers specifically to the musical genre, while hip-hop is a broader cultural movement of which rap is just one part.

In its early years, rap music featured catchy, playful, and often humorous lyrics. By the 1980s it had evolved into a vehicle for social commentary, addressing life in the ghettos, and criticising political figures – particularly the Reagan administration.

Following the demographic shift known as White Flight in the 1950s and '60s, many white residents moved from urban areas to the suburbs. Neighbourhoods like the Bronx became predominantly Black and Hispanic, facing high crime rates and widespread poverty. With limited access to music education or instruments, young people turned to DJing. They repurposed old soul, funk, and rock 'n' roll records from second-hand stores, using parks, community centres, and street corners as makeshift performance spaces where MCs added sharp, rhythmic rhymes to these beats.

By the 1980s, distinct hip-hop styles had emerged on the East Coast and West Coast. The East Coast, led by artists like Run-D.M.C., The Notorious B.I.G., Busta Rhymes, Nas, and Q-Tip, incorporated elements of rock and funk, creating a gritty, street-conscious sound. The Boom Bap subgenre, known for its punchy beats and socially aware lyrics, became a defining feature.

Meanwhile, the West Coast pioneered gangsta rap. Artists like N.W.A., Snoop Dogg, Dr Dre, Ice Cube, and Tupac Shakur depicted life in Los Angeles neighbourhoods with raw storytelling. As hip-hop's popularity grew, tensions between the East and West Coasts escalated, fuelled by media coverage and competition. This rivalry ultimately led to the tragic deaths of Tupac Shakur and The Notorious B.I.G., reshaping hip-hop forever.

In the 2000s, hip-hop evolved further with the rise of Trap, a genre originating in Atlanta. Defined by its heavy 808 bass and hard-hitting beats, Trap often explores darker themes. Meanwhile, the UK developed its own hip-hop variant, Drill, rooted in Chicago's Drill scene but adapted to reflect the UK's urban experience. Both Trap and Drill introduced an aggressive sonic style that continues to shape global hip-hop today.

The Breakbeats

Breakbeats originated in the Bronx during the 1970s, a time when hip-hop culture was beginning to take shape. DJs such as DJ Kool Herc, one of hip-hop's pioneers, recognised that the *break* (the section of a record where only the drums play) really energised the crowd. He developed his *Merry-Go-Round Technique* that used two turntables to loop these break sections back-to-back. Extending the break allowed dancers, later known as breakdancers, to move continuously, adding excitement to block parties.

Breakbeats quickly became central to hip-hop's identity. DJs such as Grandmaster Flash and Afrika Bambaataa refined Herc's techniques, solidifying break sections as hip-hop's rhythmic foundation. Iconic beats such as Apache by The Incredible Bongo Band, the Amen Break by The Winstons, and Funky Drummer by James Brown became essential grooves in early hip-hop. DJs searched for records with these breaks, looping and blending them to maintain energy and craft new sounds.

This breakbeat-driven approach defined hip-hop production, reinforcing the genre's reliance on beat loops, inspiring innovations in sampling, and bridging the energy of funk and soul with hip-hop's raw, evolving sound.

How to Work on Breakbeats

To play breakbeats with authenticity you need to focus on several key elements of funk drumming, such as ghost notes, hi-hat openings, and backbeat displacement. It's also important to experiment with different tunings and techniques to recreate the textures heard in classic breakbeats.

A great way to develop fluency is to break grooves down into small, reusable pieces that can be rearranged to create new beats. This approach mirrors the way hip-hop producers chop and combine samples to create endless possibilities for building unique grooves from classic breakbeat foundations.

When playing breakbeats, playing precise and dynamically balanced ghost notes is essential. Tap strokes are ideal for ghost notes, offering greater control and subtlety at softer dynamics. For accents, you need to develop a quick whip stroke using the Moeller technique. This requires an upstroke for preparation followed by a powerful downstroke for the backbeats. Adding rimshots on the backbeats enhances the groove's punch and clarity.

A valuable exercise is to apply ghost note ostinato patterns to various kick drum permutations while keeping the ghost note quality consistent. Focus on aligning the kick and ghost notes accurately, avoid flamming, and ensure the ghost notes stay dynamically balanced with the kick. This approach creates a cohesive, controlled groove.

This first exercise introduces ghost note patterns written in 2/4. Start by practicing each pattern individually with a simple bass drum on beat one. Once confident, apply each pattern to the bass drum permutation exercises below. Finally, mix and match the ghost note patterns. Begin with just the bass drum on beat one, then incorporate the full range of bass drum permutations for deeper groove variations.

Example 1a

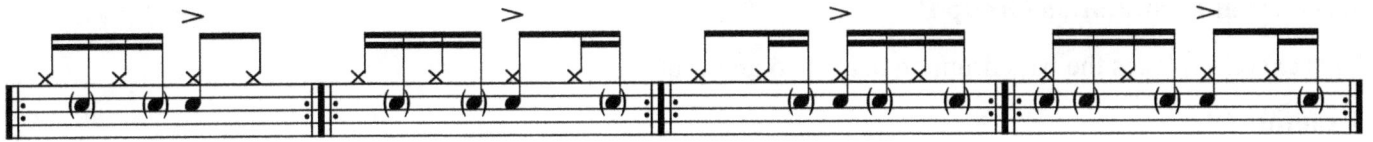

Here's an example of ghost note pattern number one played over a simple bass drum on beats one and three.

Example 1b:

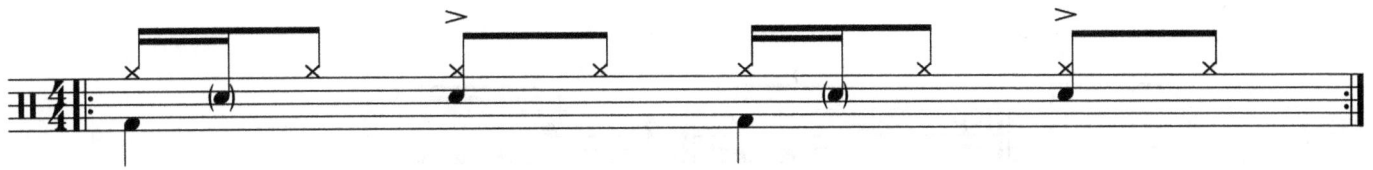

Now, apply the ghost note patterns over the bass drum permutation exercises.

Bass Drum Permutation Group A

The first exercise places the bass drum on beats one and three.

Example 1c:

Bass Drum Permutation Group B

This exercise places the bass drum on beats two and four.

Example 1d:

Start by combining ghost note pattern number one from Example 1a with each of the bass drum permutations in Group A, while keeping the first permutation of Group B steady on beats two and four.

Example 1e:

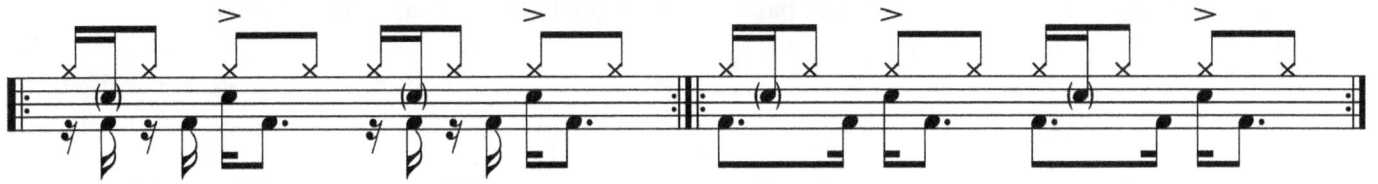

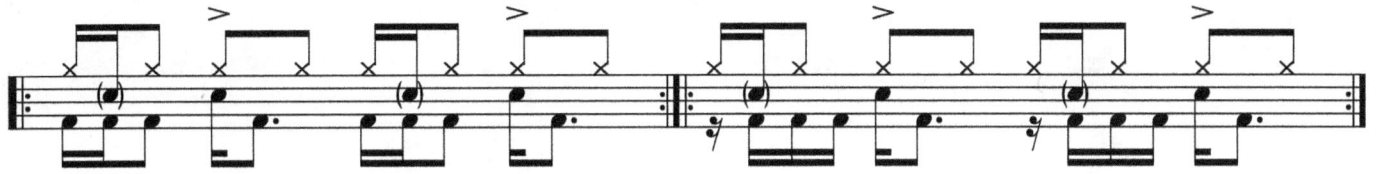

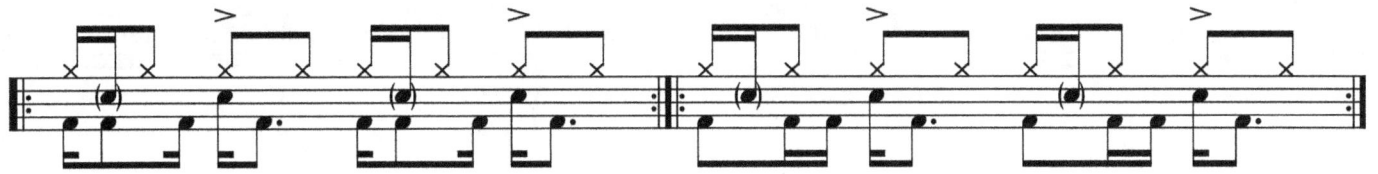

Now continue with the other ghost note patterns. Once you are comfortable with each individual ghost note pattern, combine them to create a 4/4 groove.

Here's an example to get you started.

Example 1f:

Here's how to apply the combined ghost note patterns alongside the bass drum permutations.

Example 1g:

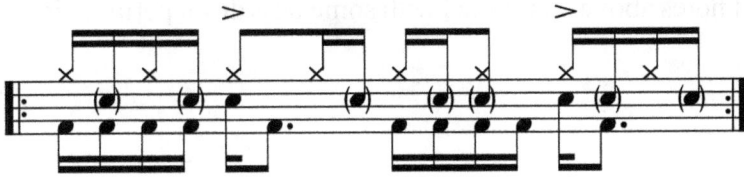

Explore the other variations, playing each one individually to maintain control, precision, and balance across all elements of the groove. Integrate them into your routine step by step, focusing on how each variation shapes the feel and flow of the beat. This method builds versatility and creativity, equipping you to apply these concepts seamlessly in different musical contexts.

Another valuable exercise is to experiment with different hi-hat patterns while keeping the same ghost note figures over the bass drum permutations. Start by selecting a hi-hat pattern that complements the groove while introducing a new rhythmic layer. As you work through various hi-hat patterns, focus on maintaining consistency with the ghost notes and bass drum placements, ensuring each layer stays clear and balanced. This approach strengthens coordination and improves your ability to adapt to different rhythmic settings, giving you greater control over the groove's overall feel and dynamics.

Example 1h:

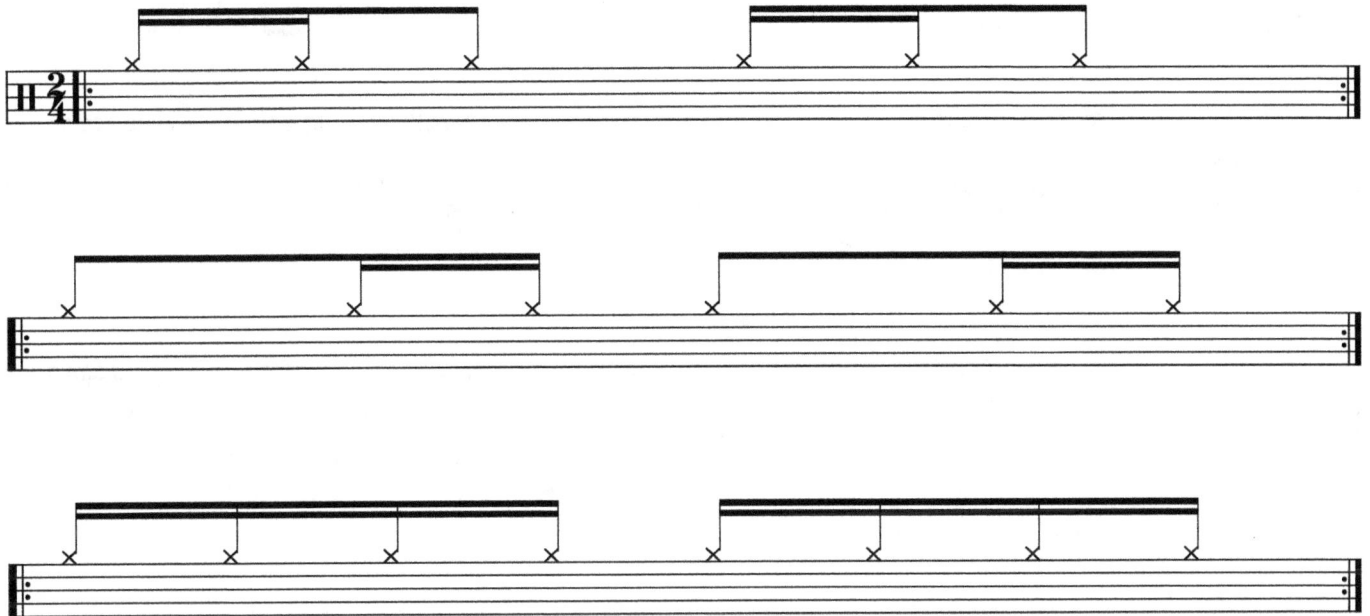

Try combining hi-hat variation one with ghost note pattern three, as shown below.

Example 1i:

Here's an example of the hi-hat variation with ghost notes above, combined with some bass drum permutations.

Example 1j:

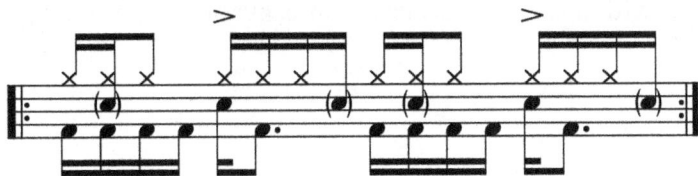

Now, continue with the other variations.

Mastering this style of groove relies heavily on controlling dynamics with precision, so strong hand technique is essential. Ghost notes placed right before or after backbeats can be tricky, and any lack of accuracy here can weaken the feel of the groove. Make it a habit to stay focused on this detail, and don't hesitate to slow things down for adjustments if needed.

Hi-Hat Openings

Hi-hat openings are a fundamental aspect of funk drumming and, by extension, hip-hop. They emphasise specific parts of a pattern, shape your dynamics, and add depth to the groove. The following exercise develops your hi-hat openings by adding them at different points in the groove. Master each idea individually before integrating it into the bass drum permutation exercise to build control.

To gain solid control over longer hi-hat openings, such as 1/8th notes or dotted 1/8th notes, start by resting your foot flat on the pedal plate. Raise the front of your foot by pivoting at the heel while maintaining stable balance on the stool. This setup provides greater precision in managing the degree of hi-hat opening.

For shorter sixteenth-note openings, the movement should be quicker and initiated with a slightly raised heel. Distribute your leg's weight between the ball of your foot and your toes, using a quick, hopping motion from the ankle to lift your leg. Land back in the starting position with full leg weight, keeping your balance steady for maximum control.

Example 1k:

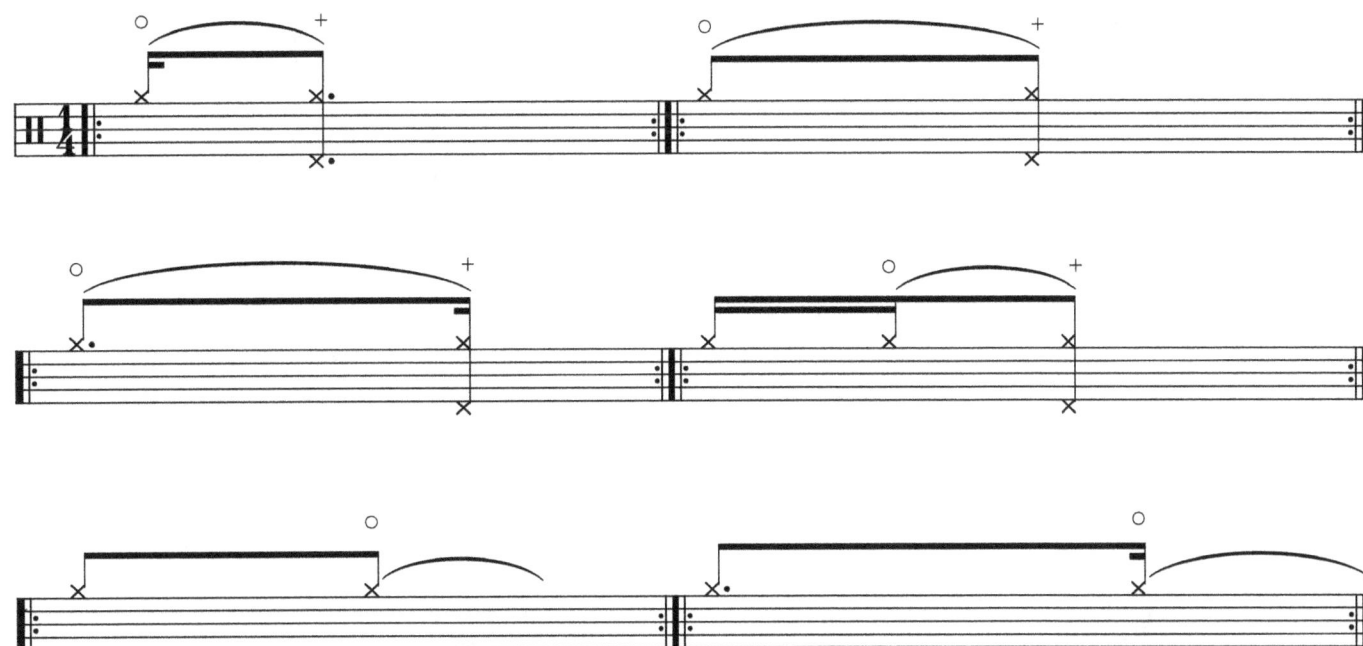

Here's an example of hi-hat opening number five played with a simple bass drum on beats one and three and backbeats on beats two and four.

Example 1l:

Now apply the hi-hat openings to the bass drum permutations. The example below layers hi-hat opening number five over each bass drum permutation in Group A, while holding the first permutation from Group B steady on beats two and four.

Example 1m:

Now, continue with the other variations.

Now it's time to bring together all the exercises covered so far. In this example, ghost note pattern number three is combined with hi-hat opening pattern number five.

Example 1n:

Let's layer this over the bass drum permutations we studied earlier. Focus on the precision of unison hits and the dynamic balance across all three voices. The hi-hat should blend seamlessly with the ghost notes, creating a shaker-like effect.

Example 1o:

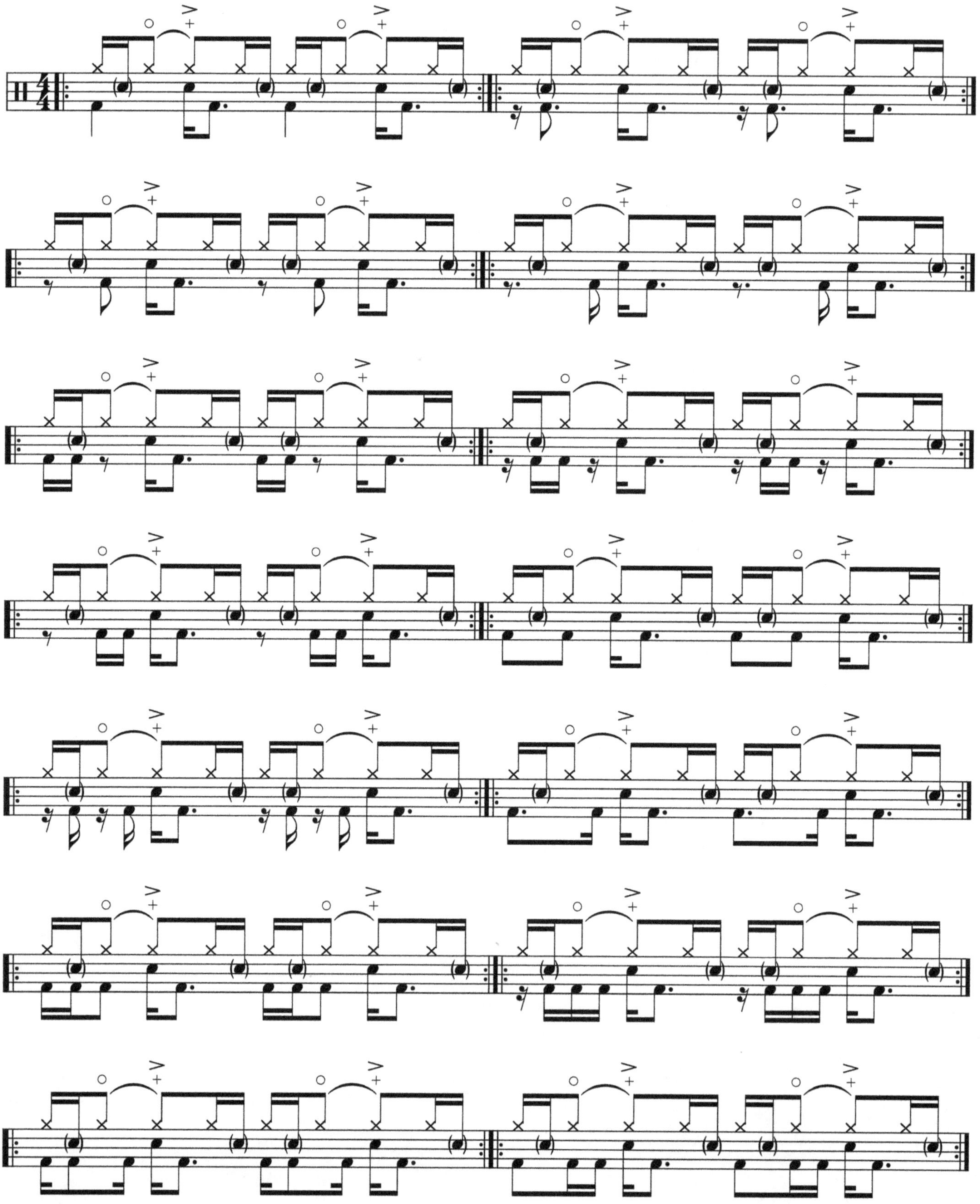

Now, continue with the other variations.

Having developed coordination between ghost notes and hi-hat openings, it's time to apply these concepts to some of the most important and widely used breakbeats.

Apache: The Incredible Bongo Band

Historical Background

Released in 1973 by The Incredible Bongo Band, Apache is one of the most influential tracks in Hip-Hop and played a huge role in shaping its sound. The groove, performed by Jim Gordon, provides the heartbeat of the song, creating a rhythm that transcends genres. Originally conceived as an instrumental cover of The Shadows' track of the same name, Apache took on a life of its own, becoming a pivotal record in the development of DJ culture. Its popularity among early hip-hop pioneers earned it the nickname The National Anthem of Hip-Hop.

DJs such as Kool Herc, Afrika Bambaataa, and Grandmaster Flash made Apache a staple at Bronx block parties in the 1970s. By isolating and looping its now-iconic breakbeat, these DJs created the rhythmic foundation for early MCs to rap over. This innovative use of the track established it as one of the most sampled grooves of all time.

The Groove

The Apache groove is built on a four-bar phrase that combines a driving backbeat with rhythmic displacements. The backbeat lands on beats two and four, but Jim Gordon introduces syncopated variations that add a sense of swing while maintaining a steady hi-hat pulse.

A key feature is its interplay with bongo rhythms, which punctuate the beat and give the track its distinctive texture. The bongos act as both a percussive highlight and a rhythmic counterpoint to the main drum kit.

Legacy in Hip-Hop

Apache has been a cornerstone of hip-hop production, sampled and referenced in countless tracks. Its infectious energy and adaptable rhythm have made it a go-to beat for producers across generations. Some notable hip-hop tracks that have sampled or referenced the Apache break include:

- Apache (Jump On It): The Sugarhill Gang

- The Adventures of Grandmaster Flash on the Wheels of Steel: Grandmaster Flash

- Doomsday of Rap: Hijack

Slow the groove down to 60 beats per minute to focus on note placement and balance between the snare, hi-hat, and bass drum. Experiment with variations on the backbeat or use the groove as a foundation for improvisation.

Once comfortable, integrate the bongo rhythms (if available) to experience the full effect of the track. Maintain a steady tempo while incorporating the displacements that give the groove its character.

Example 1p:

The Funky Drummer

Historical Background

Originally recorded in 1969, Funky Drummer by James Brown became one of the most influential grooves in music history. Though first released as a single, the track did not appear on an album until its inclusion in the 1986 compilation In the Jungle Groove, which showcased James Brown's work from 1969 to 1971. The driving force behind its legendary status is the drumming of Clyde Stubblefield, whose feel and creativity shaped the sound of funk.

The Funky Drummer break, a brief unaccompanied drum groove near the middle of the song, has been sampled countless times, influencing the sound of funk, hip-hop, and many other genres. The break demands significant technical and interpretive skill, as its intricate details are what make it so captivating.

The Groove

At around 99 beats per minute, the groove is anchored by a smooth, continuous 1/16th-note pattern played with one hand on the hi-hat. This steady pulse provides the foundation for a syncopated and dynamic snare pattern. The backbeat on beats two and four is complemented by ghost notes on the e and ah, with an additional ghosted 1/16th note preceding the backbeat.

A hallmark of this beat is the use of hi-hat openings, which occur on the second 1/16th of beats two and four, creating a syncopated, "conversational" feel that add to its complexity and energy.

Legacy in Hip-Hop

The Funky Drummer break is one of the most sampled drum patterns in music, particularly in hip-hop, where its rhythm forms the backbone of many classic tracks. Its versatility and infectious groove have been used in some of the most iconic songs in the genre, including:

- Fight the Power: Public Enemy

- Let Me Ride: Dr Dre

- Mama Said Knock You Out: LL Cool J

- Fuck tha Police: N.W.A.

Learning the Funky Drummer break goes beyond mastering a single groove and is more about understanding the essence of funk drumming. The beat challenges drummers to develop precision, dynamic control, and coordination between the hands and feet. Each ghost note and hi-hat accent must be played with intention to maintain the groove's signature flow and energy.

Start at around 60 beats per minute to ensure accurate note placement and a balanced dynamic mix between voices. Pay particular attention to the hi-hat openings and ghost notes, as these elements define the break's feel.

This groove is undoubtedly challenging, so break it down step by step. This gradual approach will help you to master the groove and apply its techniques to other material later in the book.

Start by focusing on the following exercise, which isolates the one-handed hi-hat ostinato over the original bass drum pattern, with backbeats on beats two and four.

Example 1q:

Next, add the ghost notes as follows: on the ah of beat two, on the e and ah (played as a quick upstroke) of beat three, and on the "ah" of beat four.

Example 1r:

Once you are comfortable with the placement of the ghost notes and have achieved a smooth flow and dynamic balance, focus on the hi-hat openings in conjunction with the bass drum pattern. The first hi-hat opening should be on the "a" of beat two, closing with the foot on the first 1/16th note of beat three. The second hi-hat opening occurs on the "e" of beat four, closing on the & of beat four.

Ensure that your hi-hat openings are quick, using a sharp ankle motion with the heel slightly lifted off the pedal. Make sure these openings do not disrupt the flow of the 1/16th-note ostinato or your balance on the drum stool.

Example 1s:

Once you've mastered the component parts, you're ready to tackle the full groove!

Example 1t:

The Amen Break

Historical Background

Amen, Brother was recorded by the funk and soul band The Winstons as the B-side to their 1969 single Colour Him Father. While the A-side became a major hit, earning the band a Grammy Award and a place in the Top 100, it is the B-side that has left an enduring mark on hip-hop. This is due to the six second drum break in the middle of the song, known as the Amen Break. Played by drummer Gregory Cylvester G.C. Coleman, this short solo became one of the most widely sampled beats of all time, influencing genres such as hip-hop, jungle, drum and bass, and beyond.

The Groove

The groove features a steady ride cymbal that maintains the time instead of the usual hi-hat, giving it a distinct, open feel. A delayed snare hit in the third bar introduces a syncopated twist, while a subtle gap between the bass drum and snare creates a jarring yet captivating rhythm. These elements, combined with its raw recording quality, result in a groove that is both complex and irresistibly funky.

Legacy in Hip-Hop

The Amen Break became a foundation for hip-hop music in the 1980s and 1990s. It has been sampled in countless tracks, including:

•   Straight Outta Compton – N.W.A

•   I Desire – Salt-N-Pepa

Beyond Hip-Hop

The Amen Break has been a cornerstone in other genres as well. In jungle and drum and bass, it is sped up and heavily processed, giving rise to classics such as:

•   Inner City Life – Goldi

•   Terrorist – Renegade

In modern electronic music, artists continue to dissect and manipulate the Amen Break, cementing its status as the most sampled drum beat in history.

Example 1u:

Impeach the President: The Honey Drippers

Historical Background

Impeach the President was released in 1973 by The Honey Drippers, a soul and funk band led by Roy C. Hammond. Written during the Watergate scandal, the song directly criticized then-President Richard Nixon, making it a politically charged anthem of its time. While the song itself did not achieve mainstream success, its iconic drum break made it one of the most sampled beats in hip-hop history.

The Groove

The breakbeat in Impeach the President, played by Steve Williams, is renowned for its loose, funky feel. The pattern features a prominent kick drum anchoring the rhythm, a snappy snare, and crisp hi-hats that create a tight yet dynamic texture. The overall balance between instruments gives it a warm, raw quality typical of 1970s analogue recordings.

Legacy in Hip-Hop

It has been featured in iconic tracks such as:

- Unbelievable: The Notorious B.I.G.
- Eric B. Is President: Eric B. & Rakim
- The Message: Nas

Example 1v:

Think (About It)

Historical Background

Think (About It) was released by Lyn Collins in 1972. Produced by James Brown, the song is known for the iconic drum break, performed by Melvin Parker. It is now one of the most widely sampled grooves in in hip-hop. The song was part of Collins' debut album, and while it was not a major commercial success at the time, its breakbeat would endure for decades.

The Groove

The Think (About It) break features a tight pattern that has become a blueprint for funk drumming. It is defined by its sharp, pronounced snare backbeats and the placement of ghost notes on the "e" and "ah" in the 1/16th-note subdivisions.

Legacy in Hip-Hop

Some of the most famous uses of the Think (About It) break include:

- It Takes Two: Rob Base & DJ E-Z Rock
- Let's Go: Kool Moe Dee
- Teddy's Jam: Guy

Slow the groove down and focus on note placement, ensuring the rhythm remains precise while maintaining the groove's overall feel. Then, challenge yourself by adding variations, improvising with the bass drum, or adapting the groove to different musical contexts.

Example 1w:

Synthetic Substitution

Historical Background

Released in 1973 by Melvin Bliss, Synthetic Substitution is a soul-funk track whose influence far outweighs its initial commercial success. Produced by Herb Rooney, the track gained legendary status due to its innovative drum break performed by Bernard Pretty Purdie.

The break from Synthetic Substitution fuelled the evolution of sampling as an art form. DJs and producers in the 1980s and '90s used the track extensively in their beats, making it a staple of the golden era of hip-hop production.

The Groove

The drum break in Synthetic Substitution is built around a syncopated, funky rhythm with a slightly swung bass drum pattern, which creates a groove that feels both tight and fluid. The kick pattern introduces a unique push-pull dynamic, giving the groove its instantly recognisable bounce and swing. Though seemingly simple, the groove demands control, timing, and the ability to maintain a consistent pocket.

Legacy in Hip-Hop

Its breakbeat has been chopped, looped, and transformed in numerous classic tracks, including:

- Bring Da Ruckus: Wu-Tang Clan
- Don't Believe The Hype: Public Enemy
- Straight Outta Compton: N.W.A.
- Distortion to Static: The Roots

Begin by deconstructing the groove into its components: the kick-snare syncopation, the hi-hat dynamics, and ghost notes. Pay close attention to the consistency that gives the groove its distinctive character.

Example 1x:

Chopping Breakbeats

When you have meticulously studied these iconic breakbeats and mastered their dynamic balance, feel and sound, you can begin to deconstruct them, beat by beat, to create entirely new rhythms – mirroring the approach of sampling. By isolating individual hits and fragments, experimenting with timing, layering, and pitch, you can transform them into fresh, innovative beats while retaining the essence of their legendary origins.

The following rhythmic segments from Funky Drummer are designed to be rearranged in various combinations, allowing for the creation of new grooves.

Example 1y:

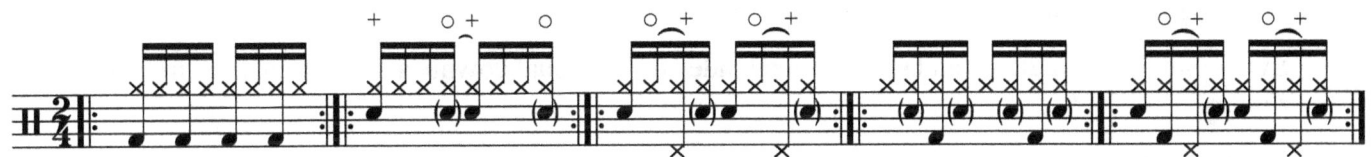

Here is an example groove created by combining the elements above.

Example 1z:

Try experimenting with this process to craft your own unique grooves, and challenge yourself to apply the same approach to other breakbeats.

Chapter Two: New Jack Swing – The Groove Revolution

In the mid-to-late 1980s, rap and R&B occupied separate musical spaces. Rap surged in popularity with artists such as Run-DMC and LL Cool J, maintaining its raw, street-level energy. Meanwhile, R&B struggled. Smooth, polished tracks from artists like Freddie Jackson and Anita Baker dominated the charts but lacked excitement. The genre had become predictable and failed to attract new audiences.

This changed with the emergence of New Jack Swing. Teddy Riley revolutionised R&B by shifting the focus to the drums – an element that had not played a central role in the genre before. Instead of relying solely on melodies and harmonies, Riley pushed the beats to the forefront. Using drum machines such as the Roland TR-808 and SP-1200, he created tight, punchy grooves that carried the grit of rap while remaining catchy and polished enough for R&B.

New Jack Swing fused elements of earlier styles and adapted them to contemporary tastes. The genre's defining characteristic was R&B-style vocals layered over a hip-hop and dance-influenced beat. The distinctive swing feel came from hip-hop drum machines and samplers of the time, combined with a modern R&B vocal style. The beats carried the street energy of hip-hop, while the melodies and vocal hooks retained the smooth essence of classic R&B.

This fusion did more than blur the lines between rap and R&B, it revitalised both, making them more dynamic and accessible to a wider audience. The style quickly gained traction, reshaping the music industry and influencing everything from fashion to film, leaving a lasting imprint on pop culture.

"New Jack Swing is a technology of music, putting rap and singing together… taking different music and fusing them all together. I was always in church, so I also had to have that church feel in my music. And that's what kept everyone on the dance floor." – Teddy Riley

New Jack Swing's identity was defined by its rhythmic complexity, with drums playing a central role. The beats relied heavily on drum machines, particularly the Roland TR-808 and SP-1200 samplers. These tools allowed producers to build syncopated patterns with sharp snares, crisp hi-hats, and deep, punchy kick drums, creating a tight, mechanised groove with a modern feel.

Live drummers translated these programmed beats into dynamic performances, adding nuance and human feel.

The drumming style in New Jack Swing focused on:

- **Syncopation:** Kick drums and snares often landed off the usual downbeats, creating a driving, infectious rhythm.

- **Swing Feel:** Though programmed, the grooves carried a natural bounce, giving them an organic and danceable feel.

- **Layering:** Producers like Teddy Riley blended live drum sounds with machine beats, merging electronic precision with natural accents.

- **Breaks and Chops:** Drawing from hip-hop's sampling culture, producers frequently reworked classic soul and funk drum breaks into fresh rhythms.

The challenge for live drummers was to match the precision of drum machines while keeping the expressive nuances intact. The style required tight timing, controlled dynamics, and a deep understanding of syncopation to maintain its infectious groove.

Impact on Music and Drumming Culture

New Jack Swing's beats provided the rhythmic backbone for artists such as Janet Jackson, Bobby Brown, and Guy, shaping hits like Bobby Brown's My Prerogative and Janet Jackson's Rhythm Nation. The genre's distinctive grooves captivated listeners and helped drive its crossover appeal.

Essentially, it redefined R&B and reshaped pop culture. From music to films like House Party and TV shows like In Living Color, its influence touched nearly every aspect of late 1980s and early 1990s entertainment. But as the genre gained mainstream success, corporate interest grew, gradually softening its raw energy and leading to its decline by the mid '90s.

Despite this, New Jack Swing's influence remained strong, shaping R&B production styles in the early 2000s.

For us drummers, it stands as both a technical challenge and a historical case study in innovation and cultural fusion.

The Leg / Foot Stroke

The leg/foot stroke combination is crucial for achieving precise, controlled bass drum articulation, particularly in the swung grooves of New Jack Swing, as the style often requires syncopated bass drum patterns that demand both speed and control.

This technique allows drummers to sustain intricate bass drum patterns without sacrificing groove consistency or dynamic balance. When applied to New Jack Swing beats, it ensures clean articulation, preserving the genre's signature bounce. Mastering this approach enables drummers to replicate drum-machine patterns with a natural, human touch.

The Leg Stroke

Position:

- Place your foot flat on the footplate, approximately three-quarters of the way up.
- Rest your heel lightly on the ground.
- Ensure the beater is positioned off the drumhead.

Action:

- Engage your calf muscles to push upward while your front thigh muscles gently lift, raising the heel.
- Hop up using a rocking motion on the ball of the foot while articulating from the ankle.
- As the heel lifts, the beater moves towards the head before being released quickly as the heel drops.
- Both the heel and the ball of the foot should land almost simultaneously, allowing the beater to strike and rebound cleanly.
- Focus on channelling energy into the ball of the foot for a controlled, articulate motion.

Steps three, four, and five happen in rapid succession. To master this action, practice it both on and off the bass drum pedal, ensuring fluidity and precision.

The Foot Stroke

The foot stroke is typically used before the leg stroke when playing groups of two or more notes like doubles, triples, or quadruples. It allows for fluid articulation and speed in rapid bass drum patterns.

Position:

- The starting position is identical to the leg stroke:
- Foot flat on the footplate, about three-quarters of the way up.
- Heel resting lightly on the ground.
- Beater off the drumhead.

Action:

- Engage the calf muscles to push upward while the front thigh muscles gently lift, raising the heel.
- Simultaneously, the foot releases the beater, then pushes the plate down while lifting the leg.
- Complete the movement by landing on the ball of the foot (leg stroke), making the beater strike the head. The heel and the ball of the foot should land nearly simultaneously, allowing the beater to rebound off the drumhead. Focus the energy on the ball of the foot for accuracy and control.

The foot-leg stroke combination is particularly effective at speeds where leg strokes alone would lack clarity or articulation. It provides a smooth and efficient way to execute complex bass drum patterns at high tempos.

Practice the bass drum combinations below to enhance coordination and precision between leg and foot strokes within a swung feel. Focus on maintaining proper technique throughout, ensuring each stroke is clean, consistent, and dynamically controlled for clarity and fluidity.

(L = leg stroke and F = foot stroke)

Example 2a:

Now that we have refined control over swung 1/16th notes on the bass drum, we can begin practicing some of the most iconic grooves from the New Jack Swing era.

Groove Me: Guy

Groove Me, the debut single by Guy from their self-titled 1988 album, is one of the definitive tracks of the New Jack Swing era. Produced by Teddy Riley, the song fuses R&B's melodic elements with the percussive, streetwise energy of hip-hop. It became a landmark in popularising the New Jack Swing sound, marking a shift in the landscape of urban music.

Groove Analysis

Drum Machine Programming: The track prominently features a drum machine, likely the Roland TR-808 or similar equipment.

Swing Feel: A critical characteristic of the groove is its pronounced swing, achieved through off-beat hi-hat and bass drum placements. This swing gives the track its infectious, danceable quality.

Prominent Kick Drum Patterns: The kick drum is punchy and syncopated, driving the rhythm forward.

Snare and Rimshot Texture: The snare drum has a crisp, high-pitched sound, with rimshots layered for added texture – a signature element in Teddy Riley's productions.

Hi-Hat Variations: The hi-hats play a pivotal role in maintaining momentum, often featuring rapid, semi-open notes that add energy to the groove. Offbeat accents create a propulsive rhythm that complements the vocal delivery.

Example 2b:

Every Little Step: Bobby Brown

Released in 1989 as a single from Bobby Brown's Don't Be Cruel album, Every Little Step is a quintessential New Jack Swing track. Produced by L.A. Reid and Babyface, the song blends infectious melodies with punchy, syncopated rhythms, making it a landmark in the genre's evolution. Its Grammy-winning success helped cement Bobby Brown as a leading voice of the era and showcased New Jack Swing's commercial and artistic potential.

Groove Analysis

Drum Machine: The track heavily relies on drum machine programming, allowing producers to create a sharp, consistent beat that defines its tight rhythmic structure.

Swing Feel: True to New Jack Swing's essence, the rhythm has a strong swung feel, adding bounce and energy to the groove.

Snare and Rimshot: The snare drum is crisp and forward in the mix, with occasional effects adding texture and rhythmic variation. The snare's placement on beats two and four anchors the groove and maintains a steady pulse.

Kick Drum: The kick drum is bouncy and consistent throughout. The intro features four-note triplet riffs.

Hi-Hat Articulation: The hi-hat plays a crucial role in creating the swing feel, mirroring the light, bouncy energy of the vocal performance.

Example 2c:

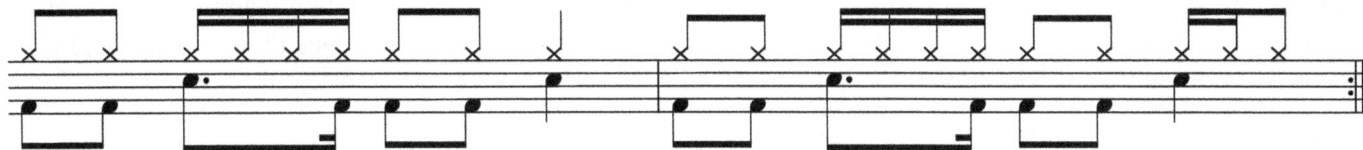

I Want Her: Keith Sweat

Released in 1987 from Keith Sweat's debut album Make It Last Forever, and produced by Sweat and Teddy Riley, the track melds the smooth sensuality of R&B with hip-hop-inspired rhythms. Its success helped launch Sweat's career, reaching No. 1 on the R&B charts and breaking into the top 10 of the Billboard Hot 100.

Groove Analysis

Swing Feel: The groove incorporates a swung 1/16th-note feel, injecting bounce and energy into the rhythm. This swing adds a danceable, light-hearted quality to the beat while providing the perfect backdrop for Sweat's silky vocals.

Hi-Hat and Tambourine Layers: The four-bar phrase of the hi-hat creates a dynamic pulse that enhances the song's movement. Additional tambourine accents and quick 1/16th-note hi-hat openings add depth and complexity.

Example 2d:

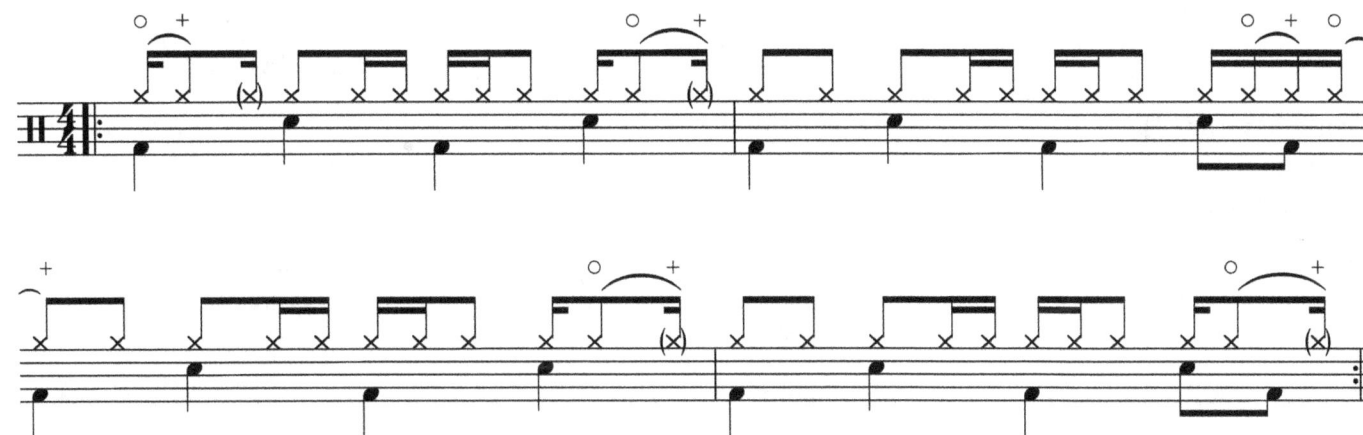

Feels Good: Tony! Toni! Toné!

Released in 1990 as part of The Revival album, Feels Good by Tony! Toni! Toné! is an upbeat, danceable anthem that perfectly captures the fusion of R&B with funk and hip-hop influences. The track's vibrant groove and energy made it a commercial success and a mainstay of the early 1990s music scene.

Groove Analysis

The rhythmic DNA of Feels Good draws a direct line to Lyn Collins' iconic breakbeat Think (About It). Producers skilfully reinterpreted the breakbeat, embedding its essence into a New Jack Swing framework.

Drum Programming: The producers adapted the Think (About It) groove using programmed digital drums, emphasising the bass drum and the swing characteristic of the era.

Layered Percussion: The groove features a tight snare sound and bright hi-hats, creating a propulsive rhythm that mirrors the original breakbeat's energy. Added elements like tambourines enhance the dynamics and give the track its unique bounce and lively momentum.

Swing Feel and Syncopation: While Think (About It) provides a raw, linear feel, Feels Good injects more swing into the pattern, aligning it with the fluid, dance-oriented New Jack Swing aesthetic. This rhythmic swing gives the track its dance floor appeal, contrasting with the stripped-down vibe of its breakbeat predecessor.

Example 2e:

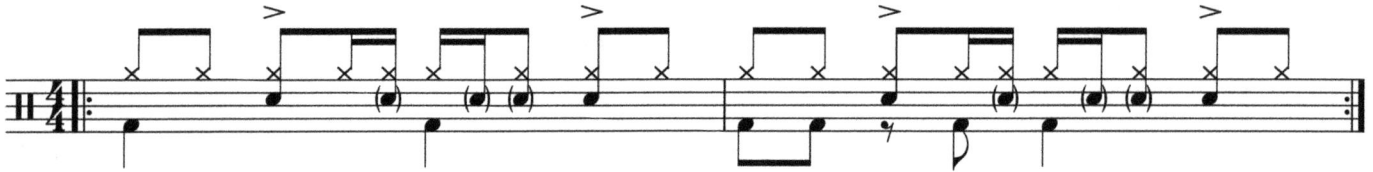

Poison: Bell Biv DeVoe

Released in 1990, Poison by Bell Biv DeVoe is one of the most iconic tracks of the New Jack Swing era. Produced by Dr Freeze, the song features a fusion of hip-hop beats, funk-inspired basslines, and pop-friendly melodies, setting a new standard for R&B groups embracing urban street culture. Its infectious groove and confident delivery made it a staple in 1990s dance clubs.

Groove Analysis

The groove shares key similarities with the classic breakbeat from Lyn Collins', Think (About It).

Drum Machine: Poison reinterprets the rhythmic framework of Think (About It) within the New Jack Swing aesthetic. The track amplifies the swing feel and incorporates more prominent digital drum programming and layered production.

Sharp Snare: The snare is punchy and forward in the mix, maintaining a consistent dynamic level with minimal contrast between the backbeats and ghost notes. This gives the groove a precise, machine-like quality, in line with the polished production style typical of New Jack Swing.

Hi-Hats and Percussive Elements: The hi-hats maintain a rapid, swung pulse, giving the groove its signature bounce. Additional percussive layers, such as tambourine, add complexity.

Example 2f:

Recommended New Jack Swing Discography

Keith Sweat: Make It Last Forever (1987)

Al B. Sure!: In Effect Mode (1988)

Guy: Guy (1988)

Bobby Brown: Don't Be Cruel (1988)

Heavy D and the Boyz: Big Tyme (1989)

Janet Jackson: Rhythm Nation 1814 (1989)

Bell Biv DeVoe: Poison (1990)

Tony! Toni! Toné!: The Revival (1990)

Hi-Five: Hi-Five (1990)

Johnny Gill: Johnny Gill (1990)

Jodeci: Forever My Lady (1991)

Boyz II Men: Cooleyhighharmony (1991)

Michael Jackson: Dangerous (1991)

SWV: It's About Time (1992)

TLC: Oooooooohhh… On the TLC Tip (1992)

Blackstreet: Blackstreet (1994)

Montell Jordan: This Is How We Do It (1995)

Chapter Three: Boom Bap – The Golden Era

Boom Bap emerged in the late 1980s and '90s, often called hip-hop's golden age. Defined by its minimalist yet hard-hitting beats, sharp lyricism, and raw, gritty sound, Boom Bap became synonymous with East Coast rap. Its influence extended beyond music, shaping the broader culture of hip-hop.

The term Boom Bap captures the genre's signature rhythmic pulse: the deep boom of the bass drum and the crisp bap of the snare. Rooted in vintage drum samples and jazz-inflected melodies, its sound revolved around:

- **Drum-Centric Production:** Using samplers such as the Akai MPC and SP-1200, producers built beats with sharp snares, punchy kicks, and driving hi-hats. Swing quantisation introduced a human feel, giving groove to otherwise rigid rhythms.

- **Sampling Culture:** Producers pulled heavily from funk, jazz, and soul records, piecing together melodic loops, hooks, and layered textures. Sampling served as both a compositional tool and a form of storytelling, paying homage to musical traditions while embedding subtle commentary.

- **Lyrical Depth and DJ Techniques:** Boom Bap emcees focused on storytelling, social critique, and wordplay, placing authenticity and lyrical depth at the forefront. DJs elevated this by adding scratching, beat juggling, and vinyl manipulation.

Producers such as DJ Premier, Pete Rock, and Large Professor shaped Boom Bap's sonic landscape. Pete Rock's jazz-inflected beats and DJ Premier's precise drum programming set the foundation for legends like J Dilla, who later introduced looser, more nuanced grooves that redefined hip-hop rhythm.

Boom Bap's Cultural and Social Impact

Boom Bap was more than a musical movement, it was a cultural force. Its aesthetic influenced fashion, graffiti and dance, while giving emcees a platform to address social issues, cultural identity, and personal struggles. The genre gave a voice to urban youth, resonating deeply within communities worldwide.

Boom Bap's Influence on Drummin

This style revolved around groove, marked by syncopation, swing, and layering techniques that reshaped how drummers approached rhythm and texture:

- **Swing Feel:** Producers such as Pete Rock and DJ Premier programmed their beats with swing quantisation, softening rigid rhythms to create a loose, organic groove.

- **Layering:** By stacking drum samples with varied tonal qualities and velocities, producers created textured, dynamic drum sounds. Live drummers adapted by incorporating subtle dynamics and nuance to replicate these studio productions.

- **Pick-Up Notes:** A defining feature of Boom Bap drumming was the use of kick drum pick-up notes placed just before the main beat, creating a distinct rhythmic push.

Groups such as The Roots helped bridge the gap between programmed beats and live drumming. Questlove became known for replicating Boom Bap grooves in live performances, showing the genre's lasting impact on drumming as both an art and a craft.

How to Work with Hi-Hat Accents

A standout feature of Boom Bap production was the use of 16 velocity levels, a function of the Akai MPC sampler. This allowed producers to assign up to 16 dynamic levels to the sampler's pads, giving them precise control over the intensity of each drum hit. By introducing subtle variations in dynamics, producers humanised programmed beats, adding movement and unpredictability to the rhythm.

Pete Rock often used these dynamics by layering hi-hats and accentuating specific drum hits. His approach gave tracks an organic, human feel, setting a new standard for nuanced beat-making. By varying hi-hat velocities, he mimicked live drumming, adding texture and complexity to his productions.

Combined with the swing function of the Akai MPC, this dynamic variation helped reduce the stiffness of programmed beats, creating a more fluid and natural groove. This balance between dynamic control and swing became a hallmark of Boom Bap, defining its rhythmic character.

The following hi-hat exercises emulate Pete Rock's dynamic approach to beat making. By focusing on accenting specific hi-hat hits, you can capture the organic feel that defines his style.

In this first exercise, the two successive accents shift forward by an 1/8th note each time.

Example 3a:

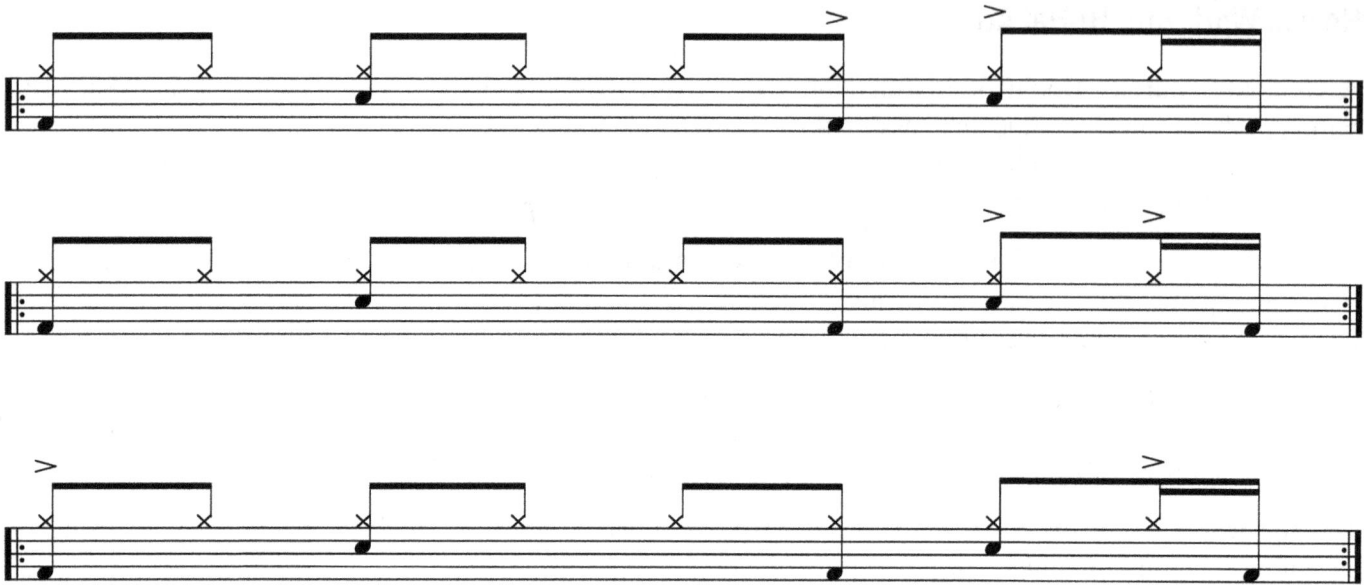

In this second exercise, you will incorporate various hi-hat figures with accents into a basic kick and snare groove.

Basic Groove:

Example 3b:

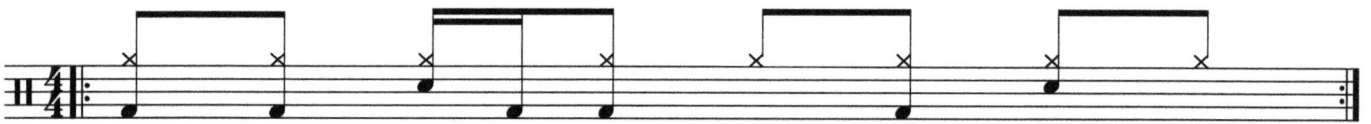

Hi-Hat Patterns with Accents:

Example 3c:

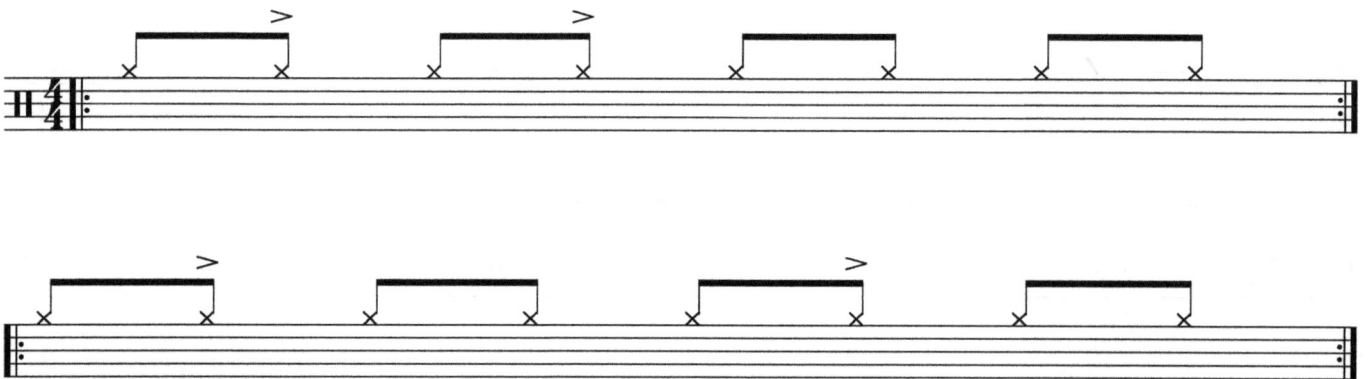

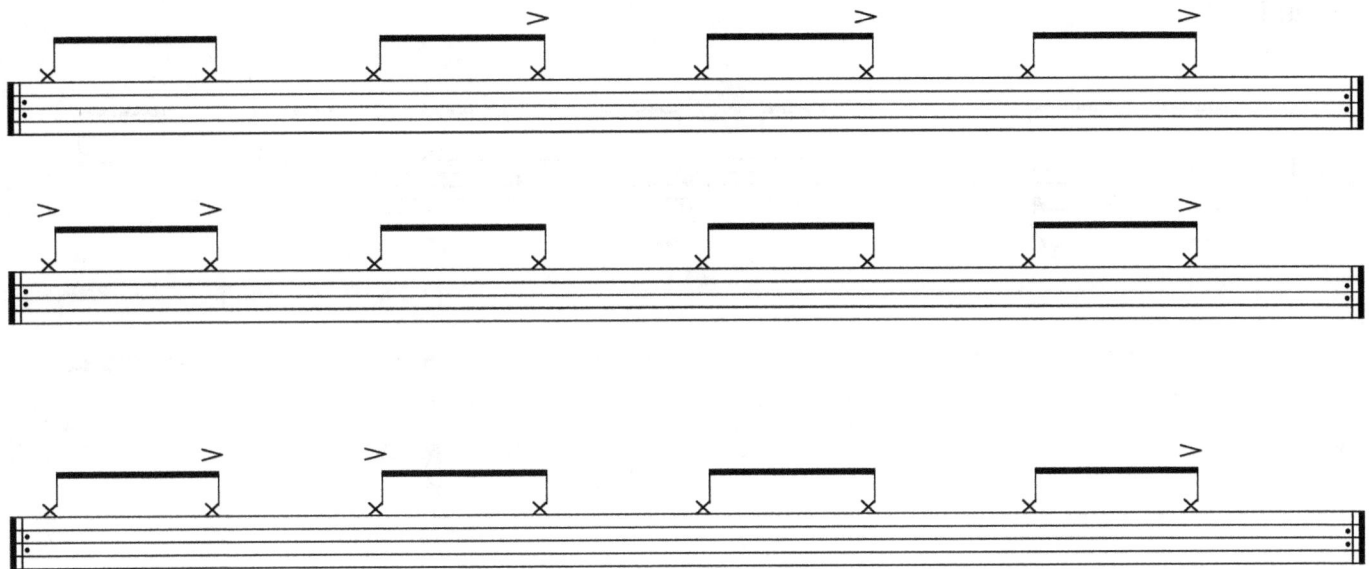

Now, let's explore some of the most significant and defining Boom Bap beats. The following grooves capture the essence of hip-hop's golden era.

They Reminisce Over You (T.R.O.Y.): Pete Rock & CL Smooth

Released in 1992 on the album Mecca and the Soul Brother, They Reminisce Over You (T.R.O.Y.) is a heartfelt tribute to Trouble T-Roy, a dancer for Heavy D and the Boyz, who passed away in 1990. This loss deeply affected Pete Rock, CL Smooth, and the broader hip-hop community, shaping the song into one of Boom Bap's most iconic tracks. With its nostalgic storytelling and masterful production, the track remains a defining moment in hip-hop history.

Groove Analysis

Drum Programming and Chopping: The groove in T.R.O.Y. exemplifies Boom Bap's production style, crafted through Pete Rock's SP-1200 sampler. Rather than looping a single drum break, he built the beat by chopping individual hits (the kick, snare, and hi-hat) from James Brown's Say It Loud: I'm Black and I'm Proud.

Snare Accent Variations: The snare work constantly evolves, adding near-improvised accents that heighten the groove's organic feel. Despite this variability, the kick and backbeats remain steady, anchoring the rhythm.

Swing and Feel: Using the SP-1200's quantization, Pete Rock introduced a subtle swing, blending programmed precision with an almost human fluidity.

Sample Use: The track's foundation is built on a saxophone riff sampled from Tom Scott's Today, featuring drummer Jim Gordon.

The transcription below condenses the most frequent snare displacement variations from the track into a four-bar phrase.

Example 3d:

Check the Rhime: A Tribe Called Quest

Released in 1991 as the first single from The Low End Theory, Check the Rhime epitomises the golden era of hip-hop. The track blends jazz-infused beats with socially conscious lyrics, creating a timeless anthem that reflects both the personal growth of its creators and the cultural landscape of the time.

The dynamic interplay between Q-Tip and Phife Dawg drives the track with their contrasting lyrical styles. Their seamless verse exchanges reflect friendship, creative synergy, and a profound understanding of hip-hop's lyrical art form. Themes of nostalgia and reflection run throughout, as the duo reminisce about their roots while addressing the complexities of their rise to fame.

Groove Analysis

Rhythmic Foundation: The rhythm section in Check the Rhime is anchored by a Boom Bap drum pattern, offering a steady yet fluid groove. One standout detail is the accented hi-hat hits on the "and" of beats two and four, which add subtle syncopation and drive to the rhythm.

Sample Integration: The main riff is drawn from Love Your Life by Average White Band, while additional samples from Minnie Riperton's Baby, This Love and Grover Washington Jr.'s Hydra enrich the sonic palette.

Example 3e:

N.Y. State of Mind: Nas

Released in 1994 on Nas's debut album Illmatic, N.Y. State of Mind is a raw and cinematic depiction of life in New York City. Produced by DJ Premier, the track captures the struggles, dangers, and aspirations of urban life through vivid storytelling. It has become an anthem for authenticity and lyrical excellence in hip-hop.

Groove Analysis

Drum Programming: The drums maintain a gritty, unpolished feel, perfectly matching the track's raw energy. The hi-hats are understated but effective, providing a steady foundation that complements the syncopated snare and kick pattern. The use of space within the beat allows Nas's complex rhymes to shine.

Sampling: The instrumental is built around a haunting piano loop sampled from Joe Chambers' Mind Rain.

Example 3f:

Distortion to Static: The Roots

Released in 1994 on their debut studio album Do You Want More?!!!??!, Distortion to Static exemplifies The Roots' unique approach to blending live instrumentation with the stylistic hallmarks of Boom Bap. The track showcases the group's distinctively organic sound, where the rhythm and groove pay homage to hip-hop's sampling tradition while being performed live. It stands as a landmark in The Roots' career.

Groove Analysis

Live Drum Interpretation: One of the defining features of Distortion to Static is Questlove's live drumming, which mirrors the cadence and swing of a classic Boom Bap drum machine. His performance draws on the breakbeat from Melvin Bliss's Synthetic Substitution, covered earlier in this book.

Sound and Feel: Questlove's mastery is evident in how he mimics the programmed sound and feel of classic MPC-based beats. His snare hits are crisp and deliberate, echoing the punchy tones of sampled Boom Bap tracks.

Example 3g:

Stakes Is High: De La Soul

Released in 1996 as the title track of their fourth studio album, Stakes Is High marked a pivotal moment for De La Soul and the broader trajectory of hip-hop. Produced by J Dilla in one of his first major collaborations, the track balances the raw essence of Boom Bap with a forward-thinking production style. It critiques the commercialisation of hip-hop, materialism, and societal ills while showcasing a production approach that would go on to influence generations of artists.

Groove Analysis

Drum Programming: J Dilla's signature touch is evident in this production. The track is built around an unusual three-bar drum phrase that maintains a characteristic Boom Bap feel but with Dilla's signature looseness. His approach lends an organic, human touch to the rhythm, avoiding overly rigid patterns and creating a groove that feels alive.

Sampling: The instrumental foundation of the track is built on masterful sample manipulation. Dilla flips Swahili Land by Ahmad Jamal, adding its warm, jazzy tones to create a lush, introspective backdrop. He also weaves in vocal snippets from James Brown's Mind the Power, adding rhythmic and thematic depth to the track.

Influence and Legac

Stakes Is High stands as an anthem for conscious rap, capturing the tensions of hip-hop's mid-1990s identity crisis. De La Soul reaffirmed their position as pioneers of alternative hip-hop, addressing pressing social issues with intellectual depth and sincerity. J Dilla's production not only reinforced the group's narrative but also hinted at a new direction for the genre – one that would increasingly embrace soulful, jazz-infused textures and experimental techniques.

Example 3h:

Drop-Outs

In hip-hop production, brief interruptions in the drum pattern, where the beat momentarily stops before returning, create dynamic tension and rhythmic variation. Known as a beat drop-out, break, or cut-off, this technique adds contrast within a track, allowing vocals, samples, or melodic lines to stand out.

This approach works particularly well for transitions between sections or to highlight key lyrical moments. Producers such as J Dilla, DJ Premier, and Pete Rock frequently used this technique, showcasing its versatility and lasting impact on hip-hop's evolution. By playing with silence and space, the beat drop-out becomes a tool for both tension and release.

The following exercises explore the drop-out technique using the three-bar groove from Stakes Is High. Focus on keeping a steady tempo and strengthening your internal timing while experimenting with rhythmic creativity.

Key Variations:

Practice keeping the hi-hat pattern constant throughout the drop-out for continuity. Alternatively, leave the space completely silent during the drop-out to emphasise the absence of sound.

Begin with shorter drop-outs lasting two beats and progressively extend them, building up to a drop-out that spans nearly two full bars.

Practice Tips:

Use a metronome to help internalise the timing and explore different settings by placing the click on:

- 1/8th notes
- 1/4 notes
- Only on beats one and three
- Only on beats three and four
- Only on beat one
- During the drop-out space to internalise the groove

Mime the missing beats during the drop-out to reinforce your sense of timing and maintain a connection to the groove.

The following exercises will improve your skill in manipulating silence and sound creatively, while remaining locked into the rhythm.

Example 3i:

Example 3j

Example 3k:

Example 3l:

Example 3m:

Example 3n:

Example 3o:

Recommended Boom Bap Discography

A Tribe Called Quest: The Low End Theory (1991)

Pete Rock & CL Smooth: Mecca and the Soul Brother (1992)

Gang Starr: Daily Operation (1992)

Wu-Tang Clan: Enter the Wu-Tang (36 Chambers) (1993)

Nas: Illmatic (1994)

Notorious B.I.G.: Ready to Die (1994)

Mobb Deep: The Infamous (1995)

The Roots: Do You Want More?!!!??! (1995)

The Pharcyde: Labcabincalifornia (1995)

De La Soul: Stakes Is High (1996)

Jay-Z: Reasonable Doubt (1996)

Mos Def & Talib Kweli: Black Star (1998)

Slum Village: Fantastic Vol. 2 (2000)

Common: Like Water for Chocolate (2000)

J Dilla: Donuts (2006)

Joey Bada$$: 1999 (2012)

A modern tribute to Boom Bap's golden era.

Chapter Four: The Influence of J Dilla

James Dewitt Yancey, better known as J Dilla, remains one of hip-hop's most influential figures. His revolutionary approach to music production reshaped rhythm and sampling in ways that continue to inspire artists across genres. Born and raised in Detroit, Michigan, he developed a distinctive style that pushed the boundaries of groove and feel. His passing in 2006 at just 32 years old has only deepened the reverence for his work.

Dilla's journey began under the mentorship of Joseph Amp Fiddler, who introduced him to production at his studio, Camp Amp. There, Dilla experimented with digital programming and developed a signature sound that blended innovation with deep musicality. Early success came through projects such as the Funky Cowboys and 1st Down before he gained wider recognition with Slum Village. Their albums Fantastic Vol. 1 (1996) and Fantastic Vol. 2 (2000) established him as a producer known for intricate beats and soulful compositions that resonated deeply in the hip-hop community.

His collaborations with A Tribe Called Quest, The Pharcyde, and De La Soul cemented his reputation as a production visionary. As part of The Ummah, alongside Q-Tip and Ali Shaheed Muhammad, he helped craft the sound of albums such as Labcabincalifornia (1995) by The Pharcyde, which featured Runnin', a track that highlights his seamless fusion of jazz, soul, and hip-hop. As a founding member of the Soulquarians, Dilla left his mark on albums such as Like Water for Chocolate (2000) by Common, and Mama's Gun (2000) by Erykah Badu, extending his influence beyond hip-hop into neo-soul and R&B.

Dilla's solo career took off with Welcome 2 Detroit (2001), an album that showcased his range as both a producer and vocalist. His collaboration with Madlib as Jaylib on Champion Sound (2003) blended their distinct styles into a cohesive yet experimental project.

His most iconic work, Donuts (2006), released just days before his passing, remains a landmark in hip-hop production. Across 31 tracks, the album's raw emotion and unconventional structure continue to inspire artists such as Kanye West, Flying Lotus, and Tyler, The Creator. Flying Lotus once said, "You cannot approach a beat without thinking of Dilla" – a sentiment that reflects his lasting impact.

Dilla challenged conventional rhythmic structures with a style often called unquantized or off-grid. He found a space between rigid time and a looser swing, creating grooves that felt both human and mechanical. This approach, later known as Dilla Time, became a subject of study for producers and musicians alike, including Robert Glasper, Questlove, and Chris Dave, all of whom sought to capture the feel of his unique timing.

As Dan Charnas explains in Dilla Time, J Dilla's influence is so profound that he is often described as "your producer's favourite producer". His contributions form a cornerstone of Black music, shaping hip-hop, jazz, and neo-soul. His work continues to inspire a new generation of musicians, cementing his status as a pioneer whose legacy will endure for decades.

Redefining Rhythmic Fee

Dilla did not invent the idea of multiple grooves, but he brought it into digital production in a way that reshaped how people think about rhythm. Jazz and funk drummers such as Clyde Stubblefield had long experimented with loose, organic time feels, but Dilla introduced "micro-timing" variations into programmed beats, repeating them precisely across a track. While Stubblefield might shift his snare timing in each measure, Dilla's programmed grooves maintained a consistent micro-timing pattern, giving them a hypnotic, mechanical, yet deeply soulful feel.

Dan Charnas describes Dilla Time as existing in the space between straight time and swing. Unlike traditional grooves that fit neatly into one rhythmic category, Dilla's beats blurred those boundaries. The result was a rhythmic approach that felt both unpredictable and completely natural.

Drum Set Application

The Dilla Feel can be achieved by combining a variety of techniques that reflect the complex micro-timing. Here's a breakdown of how it can be recreated:

- **Subdivision:** Exploring quintuplets, sextuplets, and septuplets can add the uneven, slightly unpredictable push-pull characteristic of Dilla beats. This approach recreates the subtle quantization on 1/8th notes, typically set between 50% and 65% swing on the MPC sequencer. It creates a groove that lies between straight and swung, balancing on the edge of both.

- **Voice Misalignment and Flams:** By intentionally misaligning drum voices such as the snare, kick, and hi-hats, or incorporating flams, drummers can create a feel that coexists between half swing and straight.

- **Combining Subdivisions and Flams:** For a richer rhythmic palette, blending these techniques will enhance the groove's depth and complexity.

With these methods, we can explore the unique rhythmic spaces pioneered by J Dilla. This is where precision meets imperfection and swung grooves meets straight.

Swing Percentage and Subdivisions

Imagine having a way to control the degree of swing in your groove, much like adjusting the swing percentage on an MPC. Understanding and using this concept is essential for developing feel and rhythmic control. Training your ear through active listening and analysis builds the ability to recognise and replicate subtle variations in swing with precision.

A great example of this feel is Nag Champa by Common, produced by J Dilla on Like Water for Chocolate. The track highlights Dilla's signature laid-back groove, where the swing is neither perfectly straight nor traditionally swung, making it the ideal study for mastering the feel of "drunk beats."

Example 4a

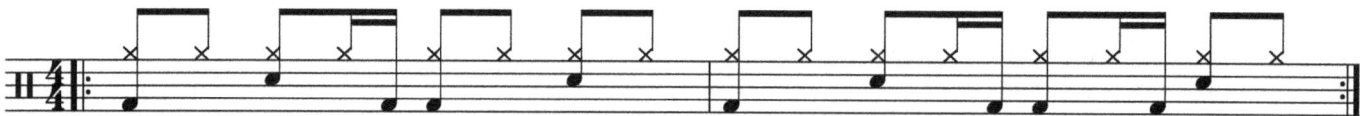

The groove demonstrates a subtle swing, beginning at a foundational 50% but shifting toward 55%, creating a slightly drunken, off-kilter feel. This minor adjustment may not be immediately obvious to all listeners, but it plays a crucial role in defining the groove's character.

Traditional notation often struggles to capture these nuances, as micro-timing details are difficult to represent clearly. This is where subdivisions become an essential tool for understanding and playing swing.

Think of subdivisions as the rhythmic equivalent of screen resolution. The finer the divisions, the sharper and more detailed the groove becomes. High-resolution subdivisions, such as quintuplets or septuplets, allow for greater precision when capturing micro-timing shifts, helping drummers articulate subtle variations more effectively.

Modern drumming relies heavily on subdivisions, yet they are often taught in ways that feel disconnected from real musical application. The key is to move beyond a purely mathematical approach and internalise the feel through consistent practice, focused study, and attentive listening. This process develops an intuitive grasp of swing, allowing drummers to blend technical precision with musical expressiveness.

Quintuplet Subdivision

Quintuplets divide the beat into five equal parts, creating a unique rhythmic feel that sits between straight 1/16th notes and the swung feel of triplets. This subdivision serves as an effective middle ground for rhythmic phrasing.

Incorporating quintuplets adds flexibility to the groove, allowing drummers to explore fluid micro-timing that bridges the gap between rigid quantisation and natural rhythmic flow.

Straight 1/16ths

Example 4b:

| 1 | e | + | a | 2 | e | + | a | 3 | e | + | a | 4 | e | + | a |

Swung 1/16ths

Example 4c:

| 1 | trip | let | 2 | trip | let | 3 | trip | let | 4 | trip | let |

Alternatively, it can be transcribed as follows.

Example 4d:

Dilla's swing

As you can see, the hi-hat lands on the first and fourth notes of the quintuplet, while the bass drum plays on beats one and three, and the snare on beats two and four. To deepen your understanding of quintuplet subdivisions, use the permutation exercise as a reference.

Permutation Exercise with Hi-Hat Quintuplet Subdivision

Bass Drum Permutation Group A

The first exercise places the bass drum on beats one and three.

Example 4e:

Bass Drum Permutation Group B

In this second part of the permutation exercise, the bass drum is placed after beats two and four, following the snare.

Example 4f:

The following exercise combines the first permutation group (bass drum on beats one and three) with the fourth pattern from permutation group B (bass drum following beats two and four).

Example 4g:

Once you have mastered and internalised the feel of the permutation exercises, begin to experiment by combining different patterns to create your own grooves. The example below demonstrates a creative application of this approach.

Example 4h:

Expanding the Permutation Exercise with Hi-Hat Accents

The permutation exercise can be further developed by adding hi-hat accents. For example, you can practice the exercise by accenting either the down-beats or the up-beats.

Example 4i:

Downbeats

Example 4j:

Off-beats

Finally, you can create phrases by applying the same approach used for straight 1/8th-note grooves in the Boom Bap style. Accents placed at various points within the pattern add rhythmic interest and complexity.

Example 4k:

Broken Hi-Hat Ostinatos

The following five broken hi-hat ostinatos are designed to integrate with the permutation exercise, much like the quintuplet subdivision. These variations introduce notes at different positions within the quintuplet framework, creating diverse rhythmic effects.

Example 4l:

Here is Broken Hi-Hat Ostinato #1 applied to Bass Drum Permutation Exercise A, combined with the third pattern from Bass Drum Permutation Exercise B.

Example 4m:

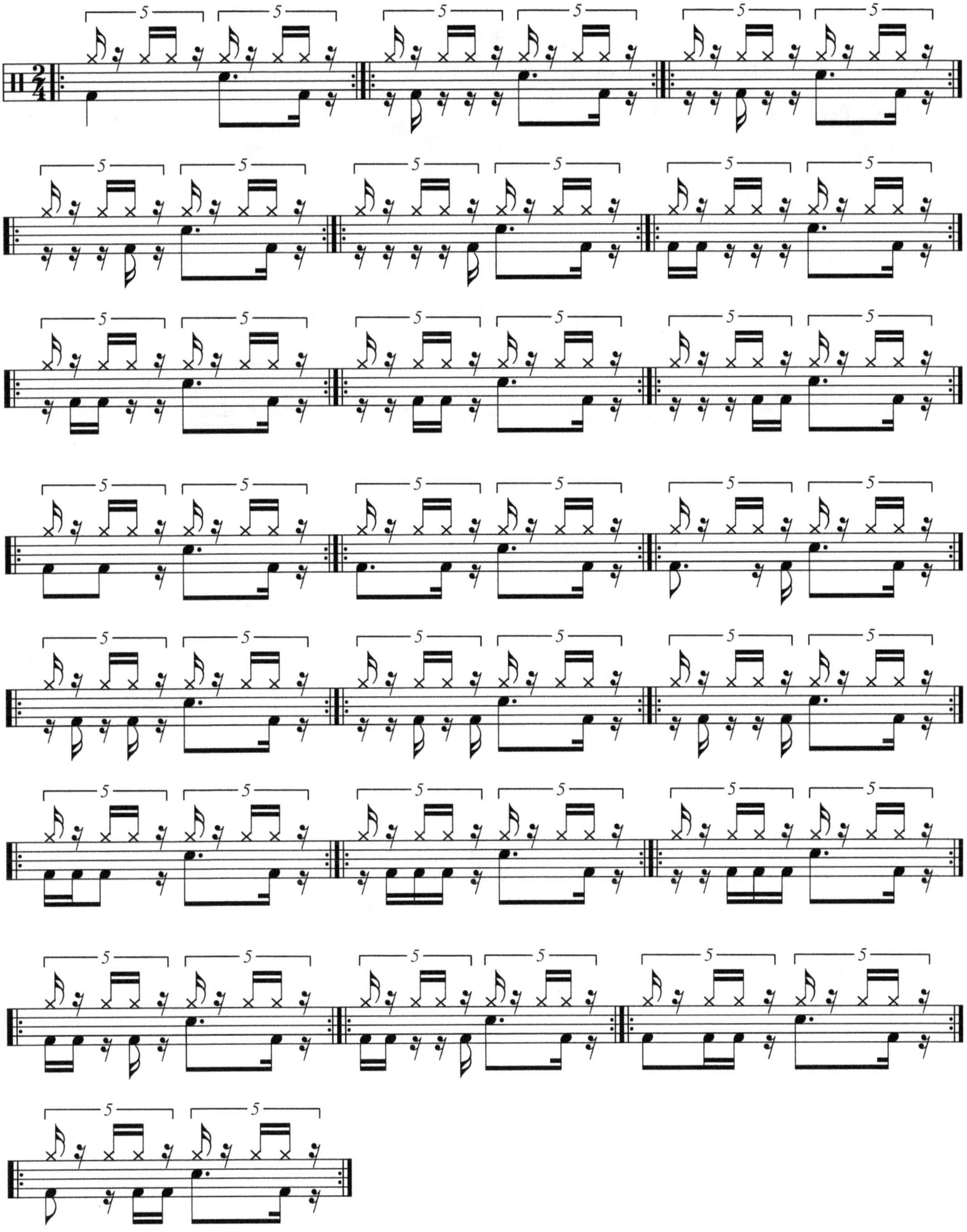

Permutation Exercise with Hi-Hat Sextuplet Subdivision

While quintuplets often provide a swing range of 55% to 60%, sextuplets extend that swing range to approximately 60% to 65%. By accenting the first and fifth note of the sextuplet, you create a more pronounced and traditional swing feel, making them a valuable tool for crafting drunk beats.

Approach this subdivision in the same way as the quintuplet exercises, focusing on precision and feel.

Bass Drum Permutation Group A

Example 4n:

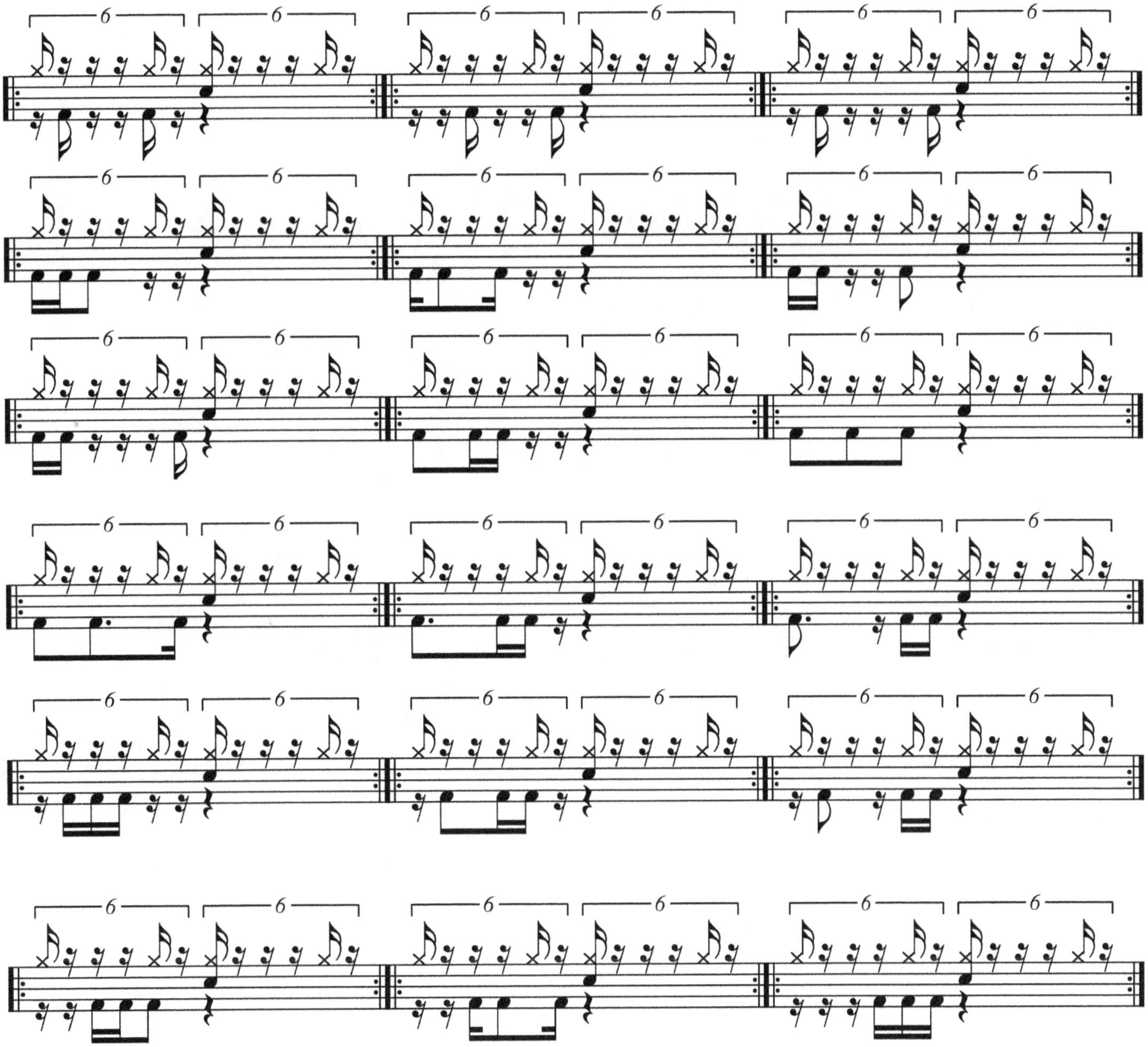

Bass Drum Permutation Group B

Example 4o:

The following exercise applies Part A of the permutation exercise (bass drum on beats one and three) with the fourth pattern from Part B (bass drum after beats two and four).

Example 4p:

Broken Hi-Hat Ostinatos

Example 4q:

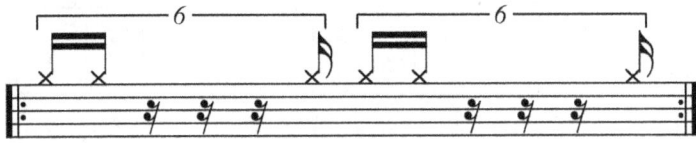

Here is Broken Hi-Hat Ostinato #1 applied to Bass Drum Permutation Exercise A, combined with the fourth pattern from Bass Drum Permutation Exercise B.

Example 4r:

Permutation Exercise with Hi-Hat Septuplet Subdivision

Because of its uniqueness, subdividing in septuplets can push the boundaries of swing even further.

As shown in the example below, the hi-hat plays on the first and fifth note of the septuplet.

By incorporating septuplets, you can experiment with rhythmic structures that are not typically found in standard grooves, expanding your versatility and understanding of micro-timing.

Example 4s:

Bass Drum Permutation Group A

Example 4t:

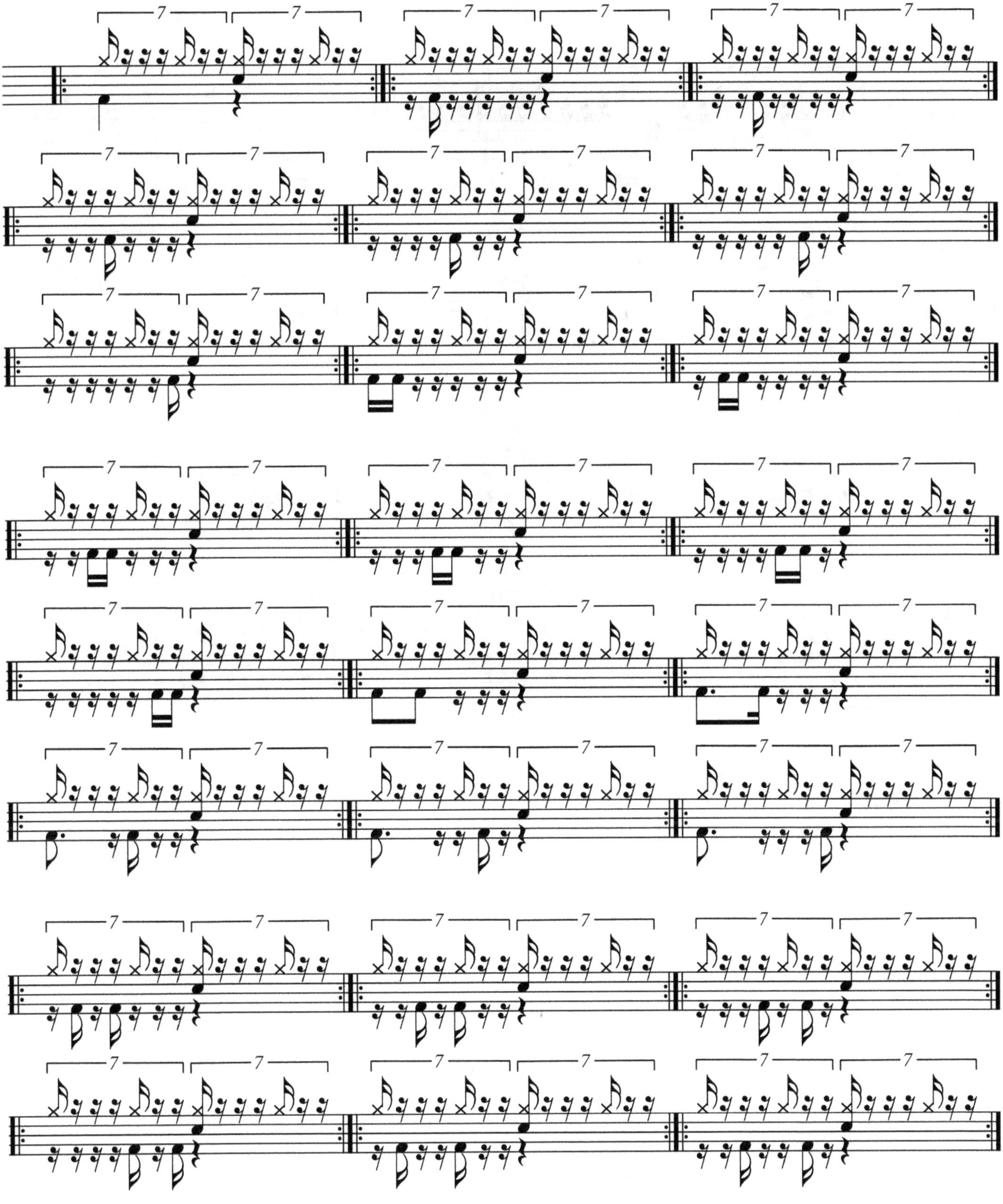

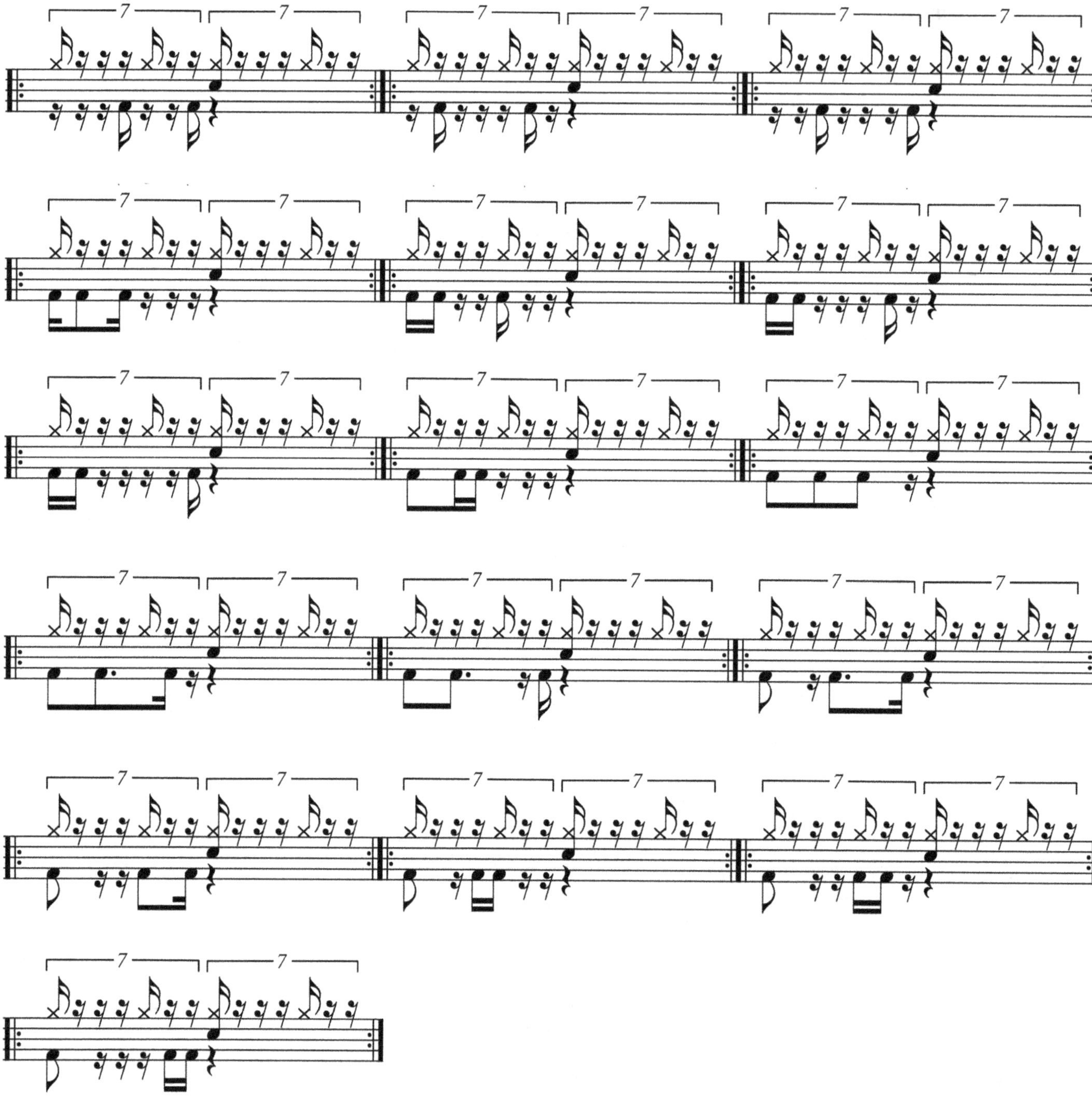

Bass Drum Permutation Group B

Example 4u:

The following exercise applies Part A of the permutation exercise (bass drum on beats one and three) with the fourth pattern from Part B (bass drum after beats two and four).

Example 4v:

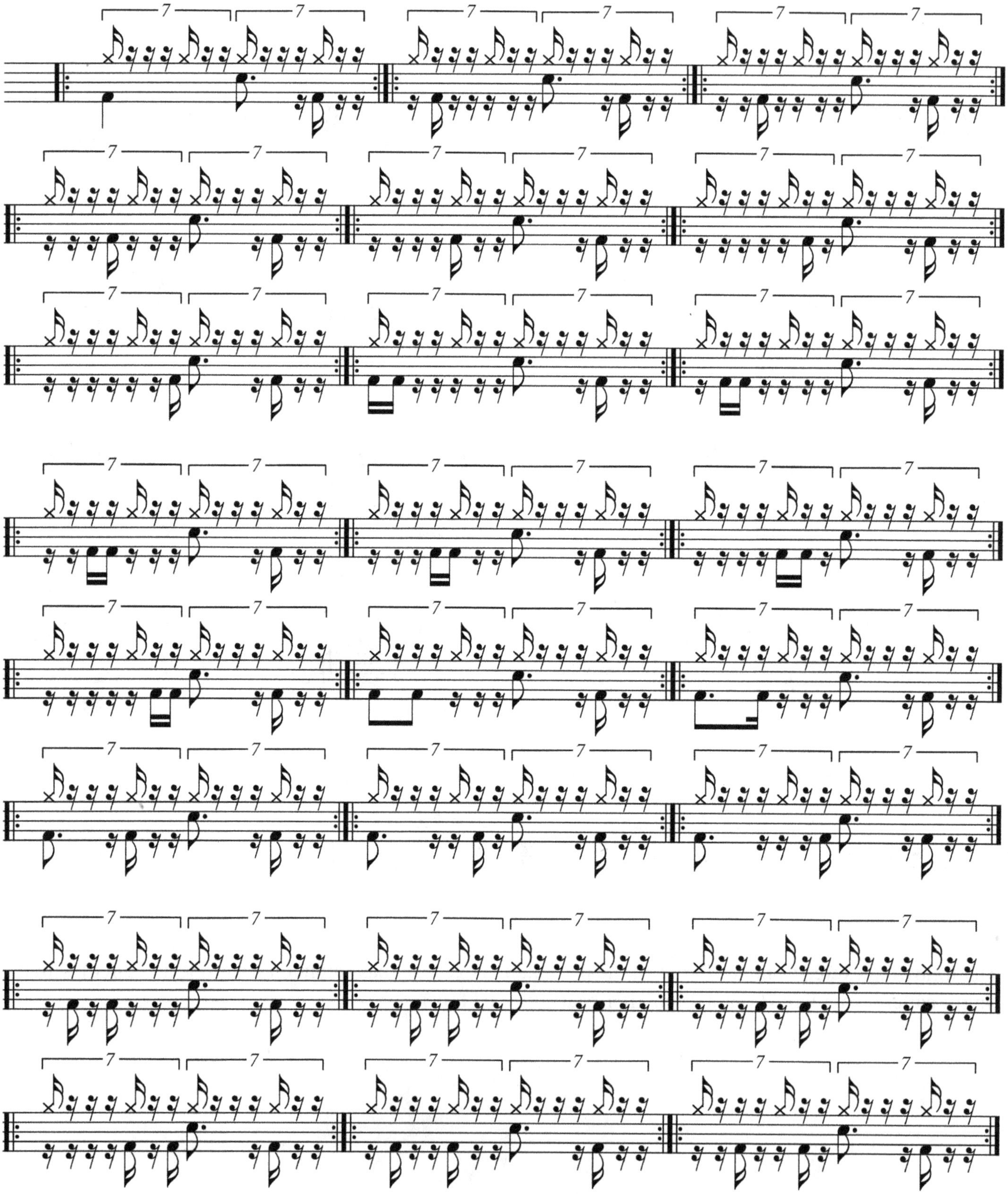

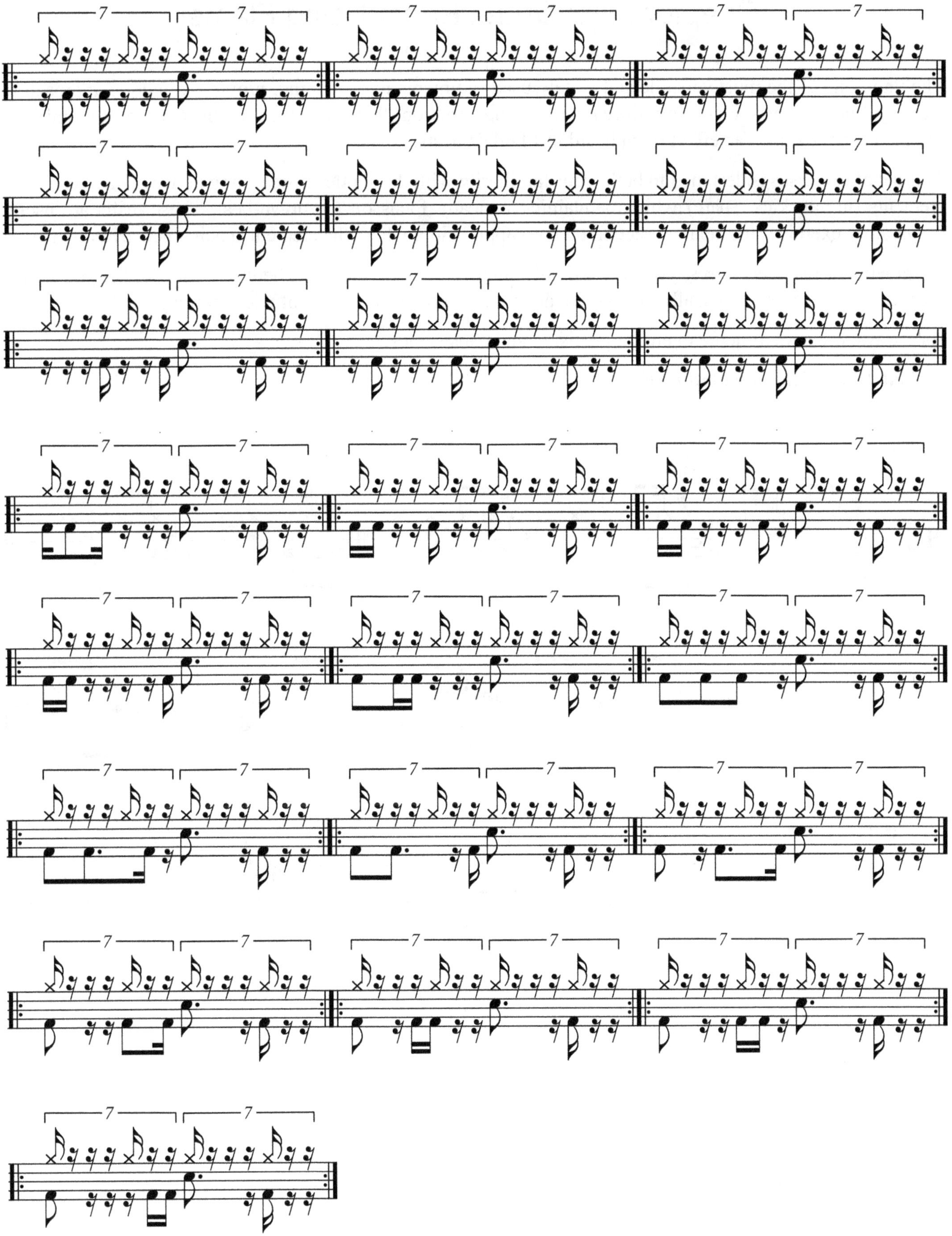
7
7

Chapter Five: Drunk Beats Using Flams

The flam, one of the most versatile and widely used rudiments in drumming, provides a unique approach to crafting drunk grooves. Flams introduce micro-timing variations that evoke the imperfect yet soulful timing of sampled drum tracks – an effect often heard in J Dilla's beats.

This set of exercises is designed to build your familiarity with the subtle, close timing between different drum elements (hi-hat, kick, snare) while maintaining a steady focus on the down-beat. These drills are useful preparatory exercises for the next section on flam application, where the element spacing gets even tighter.

By practicing these exercises, you will not only improve the coordination between your limbs, you'll also sharpen your listening skills, allowing you to accurately perceive and control micro-timing.

As always, use a metronome to ensure precision and consistency.

Hi-Hat 1/32nd Note Displacement

Example 5a:

Bass Drum 1/32nd Note Displacement

Example 5b:

Snare Drum/Bass Drum 1/32nd Note Displacement

Example 5c:

Flams: Integrating Them into Drunk Beats

Hi-Hat and Snare Flams

Execute a right-hand flam (left-hand flam for left-handed drummers), where the snare backbeat slightly precedes the hi-hat. This staggered timing mimics the slight misalignment often present in vintage samples.

Hi-Hat and Kick Flams

In this variation, the kick drum acts as the flam note, striking just before the hi-hat.

Key Considerations:

Maintain Hi-Hat Consistency

When playing flams, keep the hi-hat steady in 1/8th notes, avoiding shifts in timing or thinking in subdivisions. This consistency anchors the groove while allowing the flams to create their intended effect. A metronome must be used consistently throughout practice to ensure precise timing and accuracy.

Preparatory Drills

Start by playing unison hits between the hi-hat/snare and hi-hat/kick at a slow tempo with a metronome. Gradually introduce the flams, focusing on precision and listening closely to the spacing between notes.

Permutation Exercises with Hi-Hat/Snare Drum Flams

Example 5d:

Hi-Hat/Bass Drum Flams Exercise

Example 5e:

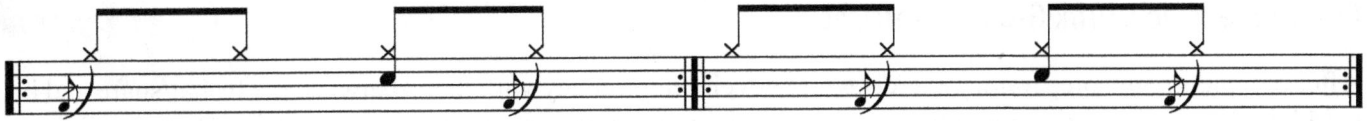

Hi-Hat/Bass Drum/Snare Flams Exercise

Example 5f:

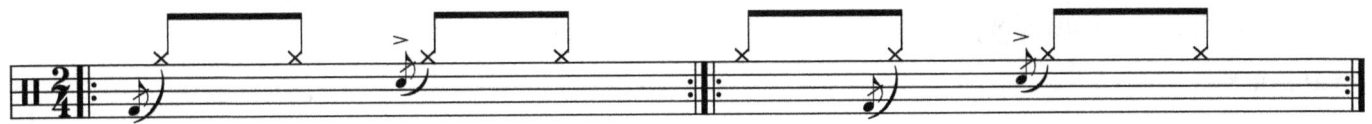

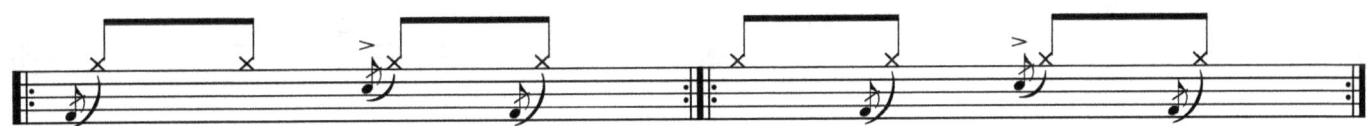

Comprehensive Drunk Groove Exercises

After completing the preparatory exercises and developing fluency with flams between the hi-hat/snare and hi-hat/kick, the next step is to apply these techniques to quintuplets, sextuplets, and septuplets. Each subdivision offers a distinct rhythmic feel.

Applying Flams to Permutation Exercises

Maintain the Subdivision's Feel: Keep the underlying quintuplet, sextuplet, or septuplet subdivision intact. The flam should function as a grace note that adds depth without disrupting the groove's foundational timing.

Ensure Consistency: Whether placing the flam between the hi-hat/snare or hi-hat/kick, maintain even spacing and consistent dynamics to preserve rhythmic integrity.

Use a Metronome: A metronome is essential for keeping time and ensuring that the subtle displacement of the flam aligns with the beat. This prevents the groove from becoming too loose or unstable.

Balance Dynamics: Unlike traditional flams, where the grace note is often played softer, in this context, the flam should match the main stroke in dynamic level to maintain groove clarity

Bass Drum Permutation Exercise Group A in Quintuplets with Bass Drum/Hi-Hat Flams

Now, apply these principles to the following exercise, focusing on precision, control, and a smooth integration of flams within the subdivision.

Example 5g:

Permutation Exercise Group B with Snare/Hi-Hat and Bass Drum/Hi-Hat Flams

Example 5h:

This example applies flams to Permutation Exercise Part A, combined with the fourth pattern from Permutation Exercise Part B, keeping the bass drum on beats two and four.

Example 5i:

Now we have applied flams to the permutation exercise in quintuplets, it's time to expand the approach by exploring sextuplets and septuplets. Take it step by step, keeping precision, consistency, and a clear rhythmic feel for each subdivision.

Simulating Electronic Sounds on an Acoustic Drum Set

Recreating electronic sounds on an acoustic kit is a great way to expand your sonic palette without relying on digital equipment. It encourages creative thinking and opens up new ways to explore textures and tones. The following techniques will help you to mimic electronic effects using just your drums and sticks!

Clap Effect

The clap is one of the easiest electronic sounds to recreate using a flam technique.

Standard Clap Effect: Play a flam starting with your non-dominant hand (for right-handed drummers, this would be the left hand), making sure the grace note is a rim click. The dominant hand then strikes firmly on the drumhead.

Stick-on-Stick Variation: Use the same flam motion, but instead of hitting the drumhead, strike your non-dominant stick as it rests on the rim. Position the stroke between the midpoint and the edge of the snare to enhance the high frequency click, making it sound sharper, like an electronic clap.

Snap Effect: For a snappier sound, use the neck of your dominant stick to strike the very end of your non-dominant stick where it extends beyond the snare rim.

Each variation gives a different take on the classic electronic clap, letting you add digital-style textures to your acoustic grooves.

Further Applications

These techniques can be integrated into grooves and improvisations. By altering dynamics, timing, and stick placement, you can simulate a range of electronic clap sounds, making your acoustic grooves more versatile and modern. Experiment with these ideas and incorporate them into your playing for a unique and creative drumming style.

Example 5j:

The Snare Drum

The snare drum is an incredibly versatile instrument, capable of producing a wide range of sounds when approached creatively. Here are some techniques to enhance its tonal variety, mimicking electronic or unconventional effects.

Achieving a Deeper, Rounder Sound

For a warmer, more resonant tone, place a dampening head on top of the snare's batter head. Products such as those from Big Fat Snare Drum soften the attack while enriching the depth of the sound.

Creating a Higher-Pitched, Drier Sound

To replicate the crisp, high-pitched tone of an electronic snare, place a small splash cymbal or bell on the batter head. This setup allows experimentation with the combined sound of the snare and the metallic ring of the splash or bell, offering a unique, layered texture.

Exploring Cymbal Applications

Resting a cymbal, such as a hi-hat bottom or small crash, on the batter head produces interesting tonal variations. Several manufacturers now offer custom-designed products that sit perfectly on the snare, enabling fresh sonic possibilities.

Utilising the Snare Wires

Snare wires can add texture to playing. Dragging a stick across the underside of the snare creates a scratching sound reminiscent of a DJ's turntable effect.

Tom and Floor Tom

Toms provide an excellent platform for experimenting with textures and tones. Here are some methods to modify their sound and develop a distinctive voice.

Creating a Compressed Sound

For a tight, focused tone, place an additional head or dampening material such as a cloth on the batter head. The type and thickness of the material drastically alter the sound, from soft, muted thuds to sharper, percussive attacks. This approach not only changes the resonance but also mimics electronic drum effects or studio-style compression.

Experimenting with Materials

Different fabrics, such as felt, denim, or microfiber, impart unique characteristics to the drum's sound. This hands-on approach to sound design helps uncover tones that are both innovative and personal.

Supporting Creativity with Tools

Many products inspire sonic experimentation. Some of the most versatile and innovative options come from brands such as Big Fat Snare Drum, New Drum Percussion, Meinl Percussion, Baldman Percussion, and Mr Muff. These products help drummers explore and refine their sound.

Chapter Six: Analysing J Dilla's Grooves

Runnin': The Pharcyde

Released in 1995 as part of Labcabincalifornia, Runnin' was shaped by J Dilla who was introduced to The Pharcyde through Q-Tip of A Tribe Called Quest. Even before he arrived in Los Angeles, Dilla had already programmed the beat that would become the backbone of the track. His approach was unconventional, deliberately off-kilter to create a more natural, human feel. The kick drum, in particular, pushes ahead of the samba sample, adding an unpredictable urgency that perfectly matches the song's theme of escaping problems and facing personal struggles

Groove Analysis

Dilla's beat on Runnin' broke away from the rigid quantisation that defined much of hip-hop production at the time. He programmed the groove to feel uneven, mimicking the push-and-pull of a live drummer. The 20-bar kick pattern surges ahead of the samba sample, which then lags slightly behind the snare, creating a syncopated, unpredictable pulse that defies conventional rhythmic expectations.

What makes this groove unique is how the kick pattern evolves. Instead of looping identically, it shifts each time it reappears in the chorus, preventing the track from falling into a predictable cycle. This departure from the standard 2- or 4-bar loop structure adds movement, reinforcing the track's loose, organic quality. The 20-bar sequence keeps the groove fresh and dynamic, building tension and energy throughout the song.

Track Creation and Sampling

At the heart of Runnin' is a two-bar samba loop from Saudade Vem Correndo by Stan Getz. Dilla manipulated the sample, stretching, repositioning, and layering it to fit his off-grid beat structure. His approach turned familiar recordings into something completely new, demonstrating his ability to craft grooves that felt alive.

The following example transcribes the first four bars from the full 20-bar sequence, highlighting Dilla's unique rhythmic phrasing.

Example 6a:

Hold Tight (feat. Q-Tip): Slum Village

Hold Tight from Slum Village's Fantastic, Vol. 2 features a guest verse by Q-Tip of A Tribe Called Quest and showcases J Dilla's groundbreaking approach to hip-hop production. The track blends sampling with organic rhythms, capturing Slum Village's soulful, experimental sound. Q-Tip's appearance bridges the legacy of Native Tongues with the fresh perspective of the Detroit trio.

Groove Analysis

This groove stands out for its subtle rhythmic details.

Hi-Hat Dynamics: The downbeat 1/8th notes on the hi-hat carry slight accents, adding depth and drive to the rhythm. This nuanced articulation is key to the groove's signature feel.

Tom-Like Snare Effect: The 1/16th notes between the second and third 1/8ths, as well as the sixth and seventh, should be played on a drum with a tonal quality similar to a tom, or a snare with the wires disengaged.

This highlights the role of sound design in hip-hop drumming. When translating sampled or programmed beats into live performance, attention to sonic details and dynamic variations is crucial. Accurately reproducing the producer's intent requires not only technical precision but also a creative approach to sound choice. These factors help bridge the gap between electronic production and live drumming.

Track Creation and Sampling

J Dilla built Hold Tight from two distinct samples. The ethereal chord progression comes from Experience in E by Cannonball Adderley, a 45-minute orchestral jazz piece featuring Cannonball's quintet. At minute 14:34, a section of electric piano chords emerges after an intense orchestral passage. Dilla extracted and looped this moment, turning it into the track's central motif.

For the rhythmic foundation, he used a loop from What Makes You Happy by KC and the Sunshine Band. He kept the intro and two-bar drum sequence intact, seamlessly integrating it with the piano sample. The result is a beat that merges disparate elements into a cohesive, genre-defining track. It's one of the many examples of Dilla's ability to reimagine existing sounds into something entirely new.

Example 6b:

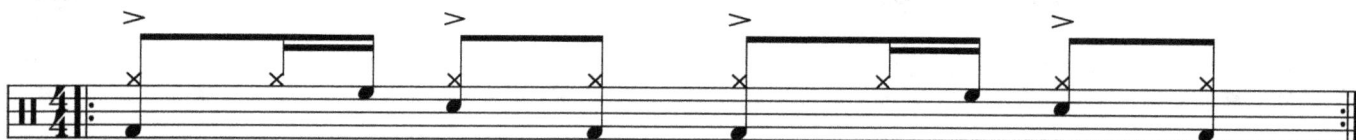

Conant Gardens: Slum Village

Conant Gardens from Fantastic, Vol. 2 by Slum Village showcases J Dilla's signature production style while paying tribute to the group's Detroit roots. The song reflects on their upbringing in the Conant Gardens neighbourhood, a historically significant area on Detroit's Upper East Side known for its suburban layout, single-family homes, and tree-lined streets. The lyrics celebrate resilience, overcoming challenges, and embracing success.

The release of Fantastic, Vol. 2 marked the end of Slum Village's foundational era. Just a month later, the group released a rare 10-track EP under the alias J-88, titled Best Kept Secret. This project acted as a bridge between their signature sound and future directions.

Groove Analysis

The groove in Conant Gardens revolves around a half-swung, two-handed 1/16th-note hi-hat pattern. A defining feature is the right-hand flam between the snare (accented) and the hi-hat (light) on beats two and four, adding depth and texture to the rhythm.

The hi-hat flam note, played with the left hand, consistently lands just before the downbeat, creating a syncopated, forward-driving feel that gives the groove its signature movement.

Track Creation and Sampling

This track is a masterclass in sampling, blending elements from eight different recordings. The bassline loop is taken from A Tribute to Wes by Little Beaver, providing a steady groove that anchors the track. The Motown! vocal sample, heard in the intro, is lifted from Award Tour by A Tribe Called Quest, further cementing the track's connection to hip-hop's rich musical lineage.

Example 6c:

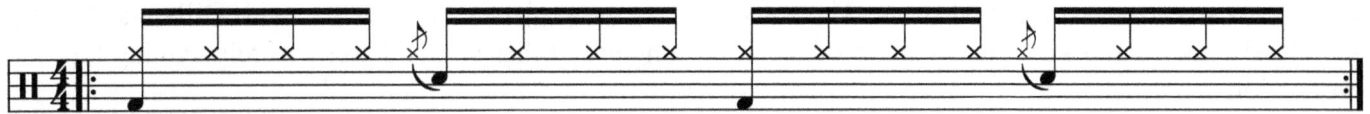

Players: Slum Village

Players from Fantastic, Vol. 2 by Slum Village was released in 2000, following the group's 1997 debut, Fan-Tas-Tic Vol. 1, which did not see an official release until 2006. Many tracks on Fantastic, Vol. 2 were reworked versions of earlier songs, refined to match the group's evolving artistic vision.

Groove Analysis

Dilla built the groove in Players by sampling elements from Rapper's Delight by The Sugarhill Gang, incorporating the iconic clap/snare and hi-hat while layering his own kick drum over them. True to Dilla Time, the kick drum is purposefully imprecise, creating a humanised, off-kilter feel that defines the track. The groove's slightly swung feel and unconventional timing give it a unique flow, balancing mechanical precision with organic movement.

Track Creation and Sampling

Players is a masterclass in sampling. The vocal hook comes from Clair by The Singers Unlimited, an *a cappella* group known for their reinterpretations of popular songs. At 2:19 in their version, the word Clair is sampled, pitched down, and chopped to sound like Players. This clever reinterpretation showcases Dilla's ability to reshape existing sounds into entirely new forms.

The drum tones in Players also stand out within the album, taking a different sonic approach from the more conventional drum sounds used in other Fantastic, Vol. 2 tracks and further highlights Dilla's ability to push sonic boundaries.

Example 6d:

Starz: Jaylib

Starz is a track from Champion Sound, the collaborative album by Jaylib, the duo of J Dilla and Californian producer Madlib. Released in 2003, the album was created long-distance, with Dilla working from Detroit and Madlib from Oxnard. Despite minimal in-person collaboration, Champion Sound became a cornerstone of underground hip-hop. The album's interplay of sampling, rhymes and beats captures the synergy between two of the genre's most innovative producers.

Starz embodies the creative exchange that defined Jaylib, with both artists blending their signature sounds into a cohesive yet experimental piece. The track reflects the project's fluid nature, with Dilla and Madlib seamlessly trading roles as rappers and producers, pushing each other's boundaries and reimagining hip-hop production.

Groove Analysis

The groove in Starz is a prime example of Dilla's organic, slightly swung rhythm. His signature feel is evident in the kick drum, which consistently lands just ahead of the hi-hat, creating a subtle flam effect. Meanwhile, the backbeats on the snare stay locked in with the hi-hat, providing a steady foundation.

Track Creation and Sampling

Dilla built Starz around a sample from The Stars Are Out Tonight by Starcastle. He isolates a section at 2:36, where the rhythm drops out, leaving only an electric piano playing 1/8th notes. He then raises the pitch of the sample and filters out high frequencies, shaping a warm, textured loop that becomes the backbone of the track.

Example 6e:

Recommended J Dilla Discography

Busta Rhymes: Show Me What You Got (1997)

Black Star: Little Brother (1998)

A Tribe Called Quest: Find a Way (1998)

The Roots: Dynamite! (1999)

Slum Village: Fall in Love (2000)

Slum Village: Climax (2000)

Common: The Light (2000)

Erykah Badu: Didn't Cha Know (2000)

Jay Dee: Think Twice (2001)

Jay Dee: Come Get It (2001)

J Dilla: Let's Take It Back (2003)

J Dilla: Workinonit (2006)

J Dilla: Time: The Donut of the Heart (2006)

J Dilla: So Far to Go (feat. Common & D'Angelo) (2006, Posthumously Released)

J Dilla: Won't Do (2006, Posthumously Released)

J Dilla: Say It (2007, Posthumously Released)

Yancey Boys: Timeless (2008)

Chapter Seven: Trap Drumming: Modern Groove Complexity

The name trap originates from the term "trap house", which referred to the abandoned buildings in Atlanta where drug dealers often gathered. Over time, it became associated with the music that emerged from these environments, capturing both the struggles and resilience of those who created it.

Trap music, a subgenre of hip-hop, has grown into one of the most influential and widespread styles in modern music. Its roots trace back to early 2000s Atlanta, Georgia, a long-standing cultural and musical hub. Trap is defined by its gritty soundscapes, heavy use of Roland TR-808 drum machines, and the signature 808 bass that forms its rhythmic foundation.

Key elements include:

- Deep, booming kick drums

- Powerful sub-bass

- Rapid 1/16th-note hi-hat patterns

- Minimalistic, looped melodies that create a hypnotic effect

These features combine to produce a sound that is both hard-hitting and atmospheric, reflecting the realities of the streets while appealing to a global audience. Lyrically, trap often explores themes of struggle, ambition, and street life, giving a voice to underrepresented communities.

Producers like DJ Toomp, Zaytoven, and Shawty Redd helped shape the genre's signature sound. Artists such as T.I., who declared himself the King of Trap with his 2003 album Trap Muzik, and Young Jeezy brought the genre into the mainstream. The mid-2010s saw a new wave of trap pioneers, including Future, Migos, and Gucci Mane, who expanded its reach by blending it with pop, electronic, and global styles.

Today, trap has transcended its origins, influencing not only hip-hop but also pop, EDM, and Latin music. Artists such as Future, Migos, and Cardi B continue to push its boundaries, ensuring its evolution and lasting impact on contemporary music.

Trap Drumming

A trap drum kit revolves around three core elements: kick, snare, and hi-hat. Each plays a crucial role in shaping the genre's distinct sound.

Kick and 808 Bass

Trap kicks are deep, punchy, and low-passed, forming the rhythmic backbone of the beat. They often pair with an 808 bass, delivering booming subsonic frequencies that add weight and intensity to the groove.

Snare Drum

Trap snares are short, crisp, and snappy, acting as a defining rhythmic element. Some tracks replace the snare with a clap for variation, adding a different texture to the groove.

Hi-Hats and Percussion

Hi-hats are central to the trap sound, often featuring rapid, skittering patterns played with closed hi-hats. These patterns create momentum, driving the beat forward. Additional percussive elements, such as claps, snaps, and shakers add complexity.

Trap grooves typically sit in half-time within a tempo range of 120 to 160 BPM. Our approach mirrors the mindset of the early drummers who adapted hip-hop beats for live performance, focusing on accurately reproducing programmed grooves.

One of the defining characteristics of trap drumming is the interplay between different subdivisions within each measure. Hi-hat patterns frequently blend binary subdivisions (quarters, 1/8ths, 1/16ths, 1/32nds) with ternary subdivisions (1/8th-note triplets, 1/16th-note sextuplets). The interaction between the hi-hat, kick, and snare creates intricate, linear phrasing that gives trap beats their signature feel.

Preparatory Exercises for Subdivisions

Developing control over both binary and ternary subdivisions is key to mastering trap drumming. The following exercise builds timing precision, and will help make your transitions between subdivisions smoother and more confident.

Use a metronome set to 1/4 notes to maintain steady timing. Any sticking pattern (hand-to-hand, right-hand lead, or left-hand lead) can be applied, depending on your preferred approach.

Example 7a:

Example 7b:

Example 7c:

Example 7d:

Example 7e:

Example 7f:

Example 7g:

Example 7h:

Trap Groove Exercises Part One

In these first two-bar groove exercises, you'll be working with 1/16th-note groupings and triplets. You'll notice that the snare, instead of being on beats two and four, is now on beat three, as these grooves are intended to be played in half-time.

Example 7i:

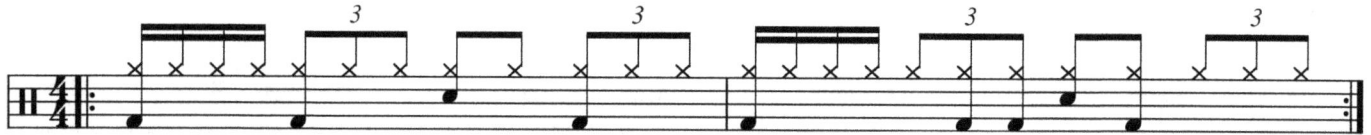

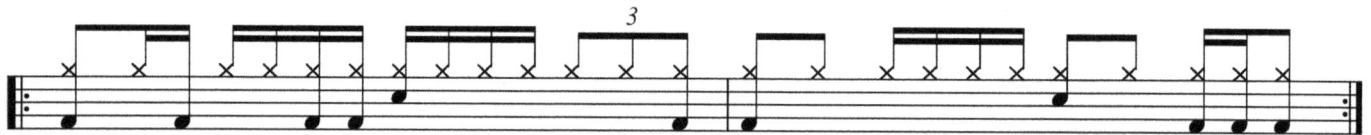

Trap Groove Exercises Part Two

In this second section, the exercises are written in a single measure, with the snare placed on beats two and four. Instead of using 1/16th notes and 1/8th-note triplets, I've introduced thirty-second notes and 1/16th-note triplets.

Example 7j:

After practicing the grooves as written and getting comfortable with the interaction between the subdivisions, take some time to experiment with different sounds on your drum kit. For example, try moving the hi-hat strokes to other parts of the kit, like stacks or rims, to emulate electronic textures.

Goosebumps: Travis Scott feat. Kendrick Lamar

Goosebumps, a track from Travis Scott's 2016 album Birds in the Trap Sing McKnight, is a collaboration with Kendrick Lamar. The song blends haunting melodies, atmospheric production, and introspective lyrics, making it a standout moment in both artists' catalogues.

The track captures the eerie yet hypnotic essence of Scott's artistic vision while showcasing Kendrick Lamar's intricate wordplay and storytelling.

Produced by Cardo, Cubeatz, and Travis Scott, the track exemplifies the collaborative nature of modern hip-hop production. Cubeatz's signature use of ambient and cinematic soundscapes sets the tone, while Cardo's rhythmic sensibilities ground the track in trap tradition.

Groove Analysis

808 Bass and Kick Synergy: The sub-heavy 808 bass forms the backbone of the track, delivering a pulsing, chest-thumping presence. Paired with the kick, the 808 anchors the groove, creating a hypnotic sense of space and depth.

Hi-Hat Patterns: Rapidly alternating 1/16th and 1/32nd note subdivisions drive the track forward. The 1/64th note hi-hat rolls, achieved through MIDI programming, can be executed using double-stroke rolls leading with the right hand.

Example 7k:

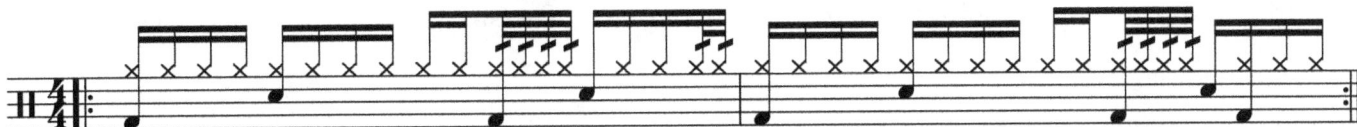

Sicko Mode: Travis Scott feat. Drake

Sicko Mode is a standout track from Travis Scott's 2018 album Astroworld, featuring Drake. Known for its unconventional structure, the song seamlessly weaves through three distinct movements, showcasing Scott's boundary-pushing production style alongside Drake's sharp lyrical delivery. The track became a cultural phenomenon, earning multiple accolades, including a Grammy nomination, and solidifying Scott's place at the forefront of modern hip-hop.

Produced by an all-star team including Mike Dean, Hit-Boy, Tay Keith, and OZ, each producer contributed a unique touch, creating a sonic journey that defies traditional song structures.

The track blends live instrumentation with an eclectic mix of samples. The opening section features a haunting organ riff lifted from Gimme the Loot by The Notorious B.I.G., paying homage to hip-hop's golden era. This sample sets the tone for Sicko Mode's ominous, immersive, and experimental atmosphere.

Groove Analysis

Hi-hat patterns: The hi-hats in Sicko Mode shift between 1/16th notes and rapid 1/64th note rolls. These rolls can be executed using double strokes to emulate machine-like precision.

808 bass and kick syncopation: The 808 basslines are central to the track's groove, combining deep, booming sub-bass with syncopated kick patterns. The kicks are strategically placed to enhance the dramatic shifts between the song's movements, emphasising both transitions and climactic moments.

Example 7l:

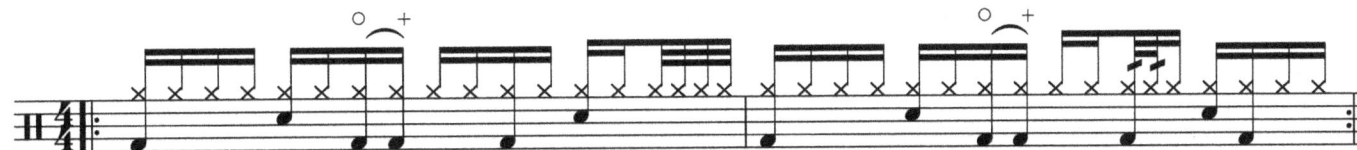

Moonlight: XXXTentacion

Moonlight is one of XXXTentacion's most iconic tracks, released in 2018 as part of his second studio album, ?. The song blends emotional vulnerability with minimalist production, creating an introspective and atmospheric feel.

Built around a looped, pitched-up vocal sample layered over dreamy, reverb-soaked synth pads, Moonlight showcases producer John Cunningham's ability to craft hypnotic soundscapes with sparse yet carefully designed textures.

The bassline is minimal but effective, consisting of sustained sub-bass notes that support the airy melody without overpowering it. This leaves space for XXXTentacion's vocal delivery, which shifts between melodic rap and introspective hums, adding to the track's haunting and immersive quality.

Groove Analysis

Hi-hat pattern: The hi-hat primarily consists of a constant 1/16th note bed, with quick bursts, almost like buzz rolls, on the "e" of the first beat and the "&" of the remaining beats.

Rim clicks: The rim click pattern is a defining characteristic of this groove, playing 1/16th note triplets on the "and" of the last beat, contrasting with the straight 1/16th notes of the hi-hat.

Beyond the main elements, the track features frequent stops and starts to accentuate specific vocal lines. There is also heavy layering, with sections where only the rim click remains.

Example 7m:

Gucci Gang: Lil Pump

Gucci Gang is Lil Pump's breakout hit from 2017, released as part of his self-titled debut album. As a defining track of the SoundCloud rap era, it cemented his place as a key figure in modern trap music.

Produced by Bighead and Gnealz, the beat is deliberately minimalist, giving Lil Pump's brash delivery room to take centre stage.

A bright, looping piano melody with a simple chord structure gives the track a hypnotic quality. The sparse arrangement creates space for Lil Pump's signature ad-libs and energetic performance. The 808 bassline mirrors the melodic contour of the piano, ensuring the low-end drives the track without clashing with the melody.

Groove Analysis

Hi-hat: Based on a pattern of even 1/16th notes, it features combinations of fast 1/64th note double-stroke rolls and 1/32nd notes that alternate within a two-bar phrase pattern.

Rim click: Highly syncopated and busy, particularly on the upbeats, it underlines the 1/32nd note hi-hats on the third beat of the second bar in the phrase.

Kick and 808 bass: The kick is tightly synced with the 808 sub-bass, forming the foundation of the track's heavy, trunk-rattling low end. The pattern is sparse but impactful, emphasizing select beats to create space for the vocals.

Example 7n:

Recommended Trap Discography

Three 6 Mafia: Chapter 2: World Domination (1997)

T.I.: Trap Muzik (2003)

Jeezy: Let's Get It: Thug Motivation 101 (2005)

Gucci Mane: Chicken Talk (2006)

Booba: Futur (2012)

Kaaris: Or Noir (2013)

Future: Honest (2014)

Drake: If You're Reading This It's Too Late (2015)

21 Savage: Savage Mode (2016)

Ghostemane: Hexada (2017)

Future: Future (2017)

Cardi B: Invasion of Privacy (2018)

Travis Scott: Astroworld (2018)

Maxo Kream: Brandon Banks (2019)

Conclusion

As we reach the end of *The Essentials of Hip-Hop Drumming*, it's worth reflecting on the rhythmic journey we've taken. From the breakbeats that laid the foundation of hip-hop to the grooves of modern trap, this book has aimed to equip you with the tools to develop confidence and authenticity in your playing.

Hip-hop may be younger than rock or funk, but it is still often regarded as a new genre, especially in drumming education. That's because hip-hop never stands still. It evolves constantly, reinventing itself with new sounds, emerging technologies, and shifting cultural influences.

This book has highlighted key moments in hip-hop's evolution, but it is just the beginning. Hopefully, it has inspired you to explore further, refine your skills, and experiment with new grooves and ideas

The exercises and concepts here should serve as a launchpad for your own creativity. Try using them in different musical settings, mix things up, and develop your own voice behind the kit.

Thank you for allowing this book to be a part of your drumming journey. Hip-hop drumming is still being written, and you have the opportunity to add your own chapter. Keep pushing yourself, stay inspired, and most importantly, enjoy the ride!

Giuseppe